SHEPHERD'S NOTES
Christian Classics

SHEPHERD'S NOTES
Christian Classics

The Writings of Justin Martyr

BROADMAN
& HOLMAN
PUBLISHERS

Nashville, Tennessee

Shepherd's Notes—*The Writings of Justin Martyr*
© 1998
by Broadman & Holman Publishers
Nashville, Tennessee
All rights reserved
Printed in the United States of America

ISBN# 0–8054–9220–8
Dewey Decimal Classification: 270.1
Subject Heading: JUSTIN MARTYR SAINT
Library of Congress Card Catalog Number: 98–21265

Library of Congress Cataloging-in-Publication Data

Bullock, Karen O'Dell.
   The writings of Justin Martyr / Karen O'Dell Bullock, editor [i.e. author].
      p. cm. — (Shepherd's notes. Christian classics)
   Includes bibliographical references.
   ISBN 0–8054–9220–8
      1. Justin Martyr, Saint. Apologies.   2. Justin Martyr, Saint. Dialogue with Trypho.   3. Christianity and other religions—Judaism.   4. Jews—Conversion to Christianity.   5. Judaism—Relations—Christianity.   6. Apologetics.
I. Title. II. Series.
   BR65.J86B85   1998
   270.1—dc21

                                                                        98–21265
                                                                        CIP

1 2 3 4 5 6   03 02 01 00 99 98

CONTENTS

Foreword vi

How to Use This Book vii

Introduction 1

First Apology 23

Second Apology 58

Dialogue with Trypho the Jew 69

Notes 86

Suggested Reading .87

FOREWORD

Dear Reader:

Shepherd's Notes — Classics Series is designed to give you a quick, step-by-step overview of some of the enduring treasures of the Christian faith. They are designed to be used alongside the classic itself—either in individual study or in a study group.

Classics have staying power. Although they were written in a particular place and time and often in response to situations different than our own, they deal with problems, concerns, and themes that transcend time and place.

The faithful of all generations have found spiritual nourishment in the Scriptures and in the works of Christians from earlier generations. Martin Luther and John Calvin would not have become who they were apart from their reading Augustine. God used the writings of Martin Luther to move John Wesley from a religion of dead works to an experience at Aldersgate in which his "heart was strangely warmed."

It is an awesome sight—these streams of gracious influence flowing from generation to generation.

Shepherd's Notes—Classics Series will help you take the first steps in claiming and drawing strength from your spiritual heritage.

Shepherd's Notes is designed to bridge the gap between now and then and to help you understand, love, and benefit from the company of saints of an earlier time. Each volume gives you an overview of the main themes dealt with by the author and then walks with you step-by-step through the classic.

Enjoy!
In Him,

David R. Shepherd
Editor-in-Chief

HOW TO USE THIS BOOK

DESIGNED FOR THE BUSY USER

Shepherd's Notes for *The Writings of Justin Martyr* is designed to provide an easy-to-use tool for gaining a quick overview of the major themes and the structure of the *First and Second Apology* and *Dialogue with Trypho the Jew*.

Shepherd's Notes are designed for laymen, pastors, teachers, small-group leaders and participants, as well as the classroom student.

DESIGNED FOR QUICK ACCESS

Persons with time restraints will especially appreciate the timesaving features built into Shepherd's Notes. All features are designed to work together to aid a quick and profitable encounter—to point the reader to sections in *The Writings of Justin Martyr* where they may want to spend more time and go deeper.

Summary. Each book of Justin's works is summarized section by section.

Shepherd's Notes—Commentary. Following the summary of the book, a commentary is provided. This enables the reader to look back and see the major themes that make up that particular book.

Icons. Various icons in the margin provide information to help the reader better understand that part of the text. Icons include:

Shepherd's Notes Icon. This icon denotes the commentary section of Justin's writings.

Scripture Icon. Scripture verses often illuminate passages in *The Writings of Justin Martyr.*

Historical Background Icon. Many passages in Justin's writings are better understood in the light of historical, cultural, biographical, and geographical information.

Quotes Icon. This icon marks significant quotes from Justin or from other sources that illuminate Justin's writings.

Points to Ponder Icon. These questions and suggestions for further thought will be especially useful in helping both individuals and groups see the relevance of Justin Martyr for our time.

INTRODUCTION

About A.D. 100, the apostle John lay dying on the island of Patmos, just off the shoreline from Ephesus, or perhaps in one of the houses of that city. Around the southwestern coastline, and beyond Cyprus to the east, an infant was born to his parents near what was once Shechem, about halfway between Nazareth and Jerusalem. His parents called him Justin, Latin for "just," or "righteous." It would be a fitting name.

What links these two figures on the stage of human history? Their involvement with kingdom work—each contributed enormously to the proclamation of the gospel message. The older man walked with Christ in his youth, was the beloved friend of the God-man Jesus, watched Him die and cared for His mother. John led the church in its glory days after the Resurrection, when believers received the Holy Spirit and went to the ends of the Mediterranean world and beyond with the good news.

John wrote firsthand accounts of Christ's life and work, explaining Him as the *logos*, or Eternal Expression of God. He suffered for his faith and was sentenced to Patmos for refusing to deny his Lord. John finished well. After his death, his writings were found to be valued by the church and inspired by the living God; his volumes became, in time, part of the canonized Scripture.

The baby Justin grew to adulthood in the area that was once called Samaria and sought to find truth in every corner. He was converted to Christianity in manhood, taught for a time in Ephesus, and moved on to Rome, where he gathered believers around him in a "philosophic" school. He published as he taught, recognizing all the while that storm clouds of persecution were building across the Roman Empire's vast reaches. The Christian faith was not legal then, nor was it tolerated. The worship of several gods was instituted as law. Pressure mounted, forcing Christians to recant or die.

Classical Apology

Classical apology has nothing to do with feeling remorse for wrongdoing and seeking restitution. Instead, it is a vigorous and noble work. An apologist gives a formal written or spoken defense or justification of some idea, faith, religion, or philosophy.

About the year 150, Justin knew the time was right to defend Christianity's right to exist. He wrote two treatises demanding a fair hearing for those who followed the teachings of Christ. Refusing to flinch at the probable backlash, he boldly addressed these to the senate and the emperor of Rome himself. In these documents, Justin defended both the right of Christianity to exist and the beliefs held by Christians. Justin is the first Christian apologist after the apostolic era.

CHRISTIAN LITERATURE

For purposes of this study, apologists were writers whose mission was to defend the faith. There were other Christian authors from the early church as well. Generally, the writings of this period are classified into four categories:

1. Edificatory, or "Devotional" (c.100–150)
2. Apologetic, or "Christianity on the Defense" (150–200)
3. Polemical, or "Christianity on the Attack" (185–225)
4. Scientific, or "Systematic Period" (200–254)

The Devotional period consisted of informal writings of faith. These authors used no pagan philosophy, no attacks against nonbelievers. These were simple, practical, discipleship materials used by the church for training and encouragement in the Christian way. They are important historical documents, showing how the churches of that era practiced their faith.

Writers from this period were generally Church leaders: *First Epistle of Clement of Rome to the Corinthian Church* (c. 95–97); *Epistle of Barnabas* (c. 119); *Epistle of Ignatius of Antioch* (c. 107); *Shepherd of Hermas* (c. 140); and the anonymously authored *Didache* (c. 70–120).

The Apologetic period writers were more confrontational in their expression. They were all trained in classical philosophy and used philosophical categories to explain the Christian faith to a pagan world. They were often addressed to the state authorities, defending Christians against false charges. They emphasized the teachings of Christ but undergirded their arguments with Old Testament Scripture.

Marcianus Aristides was the first writer of the period. He wrote his *Apology* in the 140s. Justin Martyr was the second and best known of the group. His two apologies and *Dialogue* will be the subject of this study.

The third writer, Tatian, was Justin Martyr's student. Tatian was radically opposed to Hellenism, the Greek culture; and his writings reflect this animosity. His *Oration to the Greeks* was published about 172, and *Diatesseron*, the first four-Gospel harmony, around 150–60. After Justin's death, Tatian's teachings veered from the true faith somewhat, and he became suspect by the church.

Other apologists were Athenagoras of Athens, who wrote an apology to Marcus Aurelius about 177, and Theolphilus of Antioch.

Aristides, called a philosopher of Athens, addressed his *Apology* to Emperor Antonius Pius. Aristides' *Apology* attacked the gods of the Egyptians and Greeks and criticized Greek morality. Second, the *Apology* developed the rudiments of natural theology to be used in defense of the Christian faith. Aristides called his readers' attention to the careful design of the world and to the fact of motion. He observed that whatever moves is stronger than what is moved. If we follow the chain of motion back to its source, we encounter the first mover. Aristides identified this first mover and designer of the world as the God who is revealed in Christ.

The Polemical period was a time when Christian thinkers went on the offensive against heresies and heretics. In the context of the time, this was imperative in order to maintain pure doctrine. The Roman Empire was awash in a complex, eclectic mix of mythology, mystery religions, pantheons, and empire gods. The religious culture borrowed elements from Christianity and mixed it with non-Christian beliefs and practices. Confusion often reigned.

Polemicists, therefore, aimed toward eliminating heresy. These third-generation writers, most of whom were born pagans, brought with them a strong understanding of other belief systems. The New Testament was emphasized here, and a greater consensus arose as to what constituted "orthodox" Christian thought.

Four writers stand out in this category: Irenaeus of Lyons, *Five Books Against Heresies* (c. 185); Hippolytus, student of Irenaeus, *Refutation of All Heresies* (c. 200); Tertullian, first to write in Latin and called Father of Western Theology, *Prescription Against the Heretics* (c. 197); and Cyprian of Carthage, *On the Unity of the Catholic Church* (c. 255).

The last of the four periods is the Scientific, whose writers attempted to present Christianity systematically. The first of these was Titus Flavius Clemens, best known as Clement of Alexandria. Clement was born about 150. Some believe he was born in Athens. He came to Alexandria shortly after 200 where he lived until his death in 219.

A second theologian of this period, Origen of Alexandria, was born around A.D. 185 and died in 255. Origen's volumes number more than six thousand. He wrote the first systematic theology of the church, called *On First Principles*, and a combination of polyglot, multicolumn versions of Scripture.

WHY STUDY JUSTIN MARTYR?

Justin Martyr is rightly considered the best of the early church apologists. Many of his writings have survived intact from the period immediately following John's *Revelation* and, therefore, are critical second-century links to the thought and practices of the New Testament church. Justin is not only a *defender*, however.

He was also a *definer*, who articulated theological concepts for the church when there was as yet no accepted canon of Scripture. He strongly influenced how second-century Christians defined key theological terms.

He was a *describer*, opening the windows of second-century churches to observation. Christian worship and the services connected with the rites of baptism and Communion were described with vivid detail, allowing twenty-first century Christians the opportunity to observe the life and development of the church in the second century.

He was a *dialoguer*—one who interacted with the world in which he lived. He taught, wrote, and witnessed of Christ, sometimes in unusual ways. His *Dialogue with Trypho the Jew* is perhaps the first autobiographical account of an interfaith encounter outside of the New Testament writings. Justin shared his personal testimony and argued intelligently from Scripture with a Jewish man concerning matters of faith and practice. His readers come along with him and hear his eloquent, passionate heart for evangelism.

If you were to write, would you write as a defender, a describer, or a dialoguer? Could you defend the Christian doctrine and rights of believers against today's antagonism? Would you be able to record vivid descriptions of church celebrations in worship today? Do you have an autobiographical account of an interfaith encounter to share?

How does the situation of the church today differ from the situation Justin faced in the second century? Why is a well-informed defense of the Christian faith needed in our time?

The continuing miracle of Christianity was stated by Peter in the first century: "You love him even though you have never seen him. Though you do not see him, you trust him; and even now you are happy with a glorious, inexpressible joy. Your reward for trusting him will be the salvation of your souls" (1 Pet. 1:8–9, NLT).

Finally, Justin was *defiant*. His later years were bold and challenging. Openly resistant to the empire's unjust attitudes about, and sentencing of, Christians, Justin proclaimed himself one of those who are "unjustly hated and wantonly abused." His goal was to defend the cause of Christ to the death. And that he did. In the year 165 he, with six of his friends, was denounced as a believer and taken before the Prefect of Rome, who demanded that he recant. He would not. Proclaiming Christ until the sword severed his head from his body, Justin defiantly refused to bend his knee to any but his Lord Jesus. For this conviction the church called him Justin Martyr.

PURPOSE AND FORMAT OF STUDY

The purpose of this study is to examine the life and writings of Justin Martyr. The first phase will sketch his life and times, his philosophical background, and those writings which are attributed to him: the *First Apology*, the *Second Apology*, and Justin's *Dialogue with Trypho the Jew*, a different genre of literature altogether.

The second century was a critical testing ground for Christianity. By this time, all of the firsthand witnesses of Jesus' life, death, and Resurrection were dead. What would happen with those who had received the gospel but who weren't first-hand witnesses? From a merely human point of view, Christianity's survival seemed unlikely. From God's perspective, the Holy Spirit had been given and was silently taking roots in the hearts of faithful men and women, many of whom, like Justin, would give their lives in service to Christ.

HISTORICAL CONTEXT

World Events. Justin Martyr appeared first on the stage of Christian history about the year 114, in an age of geographic and intellectual conquest. In the Mediterranean Basin, Trajan annexed (116) the empires of Romania, Arabia, and the Parthians. Hadrian settled (117) his Roman frontiers and finished plans for his wall to be built across Britain's landscape (122–27). Closer to home, Judea was soon to become Palestine, and all Jews were to be banished from Jerusalem.

With the advance of armies and colonizing of vast new territory came the dispersion of groups of people. Roman soldiers established settlements in distant provinces. Captives were pressed into slavery. Families were uprooted and sent to inhabit new colonies. Jews were once again banished from long-held lands. In the face of these unsettling times, the Roman government sought to strengthen its empire by setting up two new state religions which, it believed, all persons could accept. Old ways would slip away, the government reasoned; and in their places would stand new, imperial gods, and new ways of thinking. In the years ahead, this two-pronged strategy would cause Christians great suffering.

The first scheme was to mix together a kind of "religious stew," composed of all of the gods from each region of the empire. These, along with the Roman Pantheon, were represented in Rome's temple, and citizens were encouraged to worship them all. This gradually became accepted as people, holding dozens of religions and philosophies, mingled in the streets and marketplaces. It became fashionable to worship

Pax Romana

In the first century, the political unity of the Roman Empire was based on Roman law and Hellenistic, or Greek, culture. For almost two hundred years (27 B.C.–A.D. 180) there was relative peace in the land that stretched northward from Egypt to Britain. Well-guarded roads, like the Appian Way, made travel safe; the Greek language fostered a common communication system; and trade flourished, allowing Christianity to spread quickly.

Religious Syncretism

Religious syncretism is the haphazard mixing of religious elements from various religions. During this era, a non-Christian or non-Jewish family might worship any number of regional gods for fertility, agricultural, financial success, and physical protection.

Taurobolism

Taurobolism was an initiation rite associated with more than one of the mystery religions. During this ceremony, the recipient descended into a pit, above which was led a bull; the animal was then slain. The blood of the bull showered down on the initiate, who then "bathed" in it. This practice became well known during the second century.

Twisted Ruler

Domitian held the throne of the Roman Empire from 81 to 96. Although reputed to be a good administrator, this despot enjoyed stabbing flies with his pen and watching gladiatorial fights between dwarfs and women. The early historian, Pliny, described him as the beast from hell that sat in its den, licking blood. John's Revelation uses many of the same word-pictures.

several gods at once, something true Christians and Jews simply could not do.

To complicate matters, "mystery religions" arose as people adopted personal gods and were initiated into secret rites for cult membership. These cults often centered around myths about the origins of the world and the deities which, they believed, gave and sustained life. Some of the more popular cults were: Mithraism, a mystery religion that originated in Persia and was Christianity's greatest rival for almost five hundred years. Magna Mater, also known as the "Great Mother" religion, appealed particularly to males, and included the strange initiation rite called Taurobolism. Still others focused on such emphases as fertility rites (Dionysius Cult) or strict self-denial (Orpheus Cult).

The other plan for religious unity involved emperor worship. When Emperor Domitian assumed the throne in the year 81, he became convinced that he was a god and took for himself the title *Dominus et Deus* (Lord and God). Roman citizens were then required to worship his image at least once a year at one of many shrines newly built for this event. Throwing incense into the fire and uttering the phrase "Caesar is Lord" earned the worshiper a "libellus," a stamped certificate indicating the citizen was in good standing.

Refusing to burn incense before the emperor's image was an act of disloyalty or treason against the empire. Many Christians stubbornly resisted the emperor's demand for worship, testifying of their faith in Christ instead. Their confession that "Jesus Christ is Lord" was often their first step toward death. And yet death was never far from the thoughts of these first- and second-century Christians and churches. They had witnessed persecution often; and, since their Lord had experienced death on the cross, they accepted and even embraced physical suffering as a way of following Him.

Many issues had faced the church since the close of the New Testament period. An overview of church life, from Acts to the second century, will help put this study of Justin Martyr into perspective.

The State of the Church. After the Resurrection of Jesus Christ, the small band of disciples went to a mountain near Galilee, where they received the Great Commission, given by Christ Himself, to take the gospel into all of the world (Matt. 28:16–20).

Soon thereafter, men and women gathered in the upper room for prayer and experienced Pentecost when the Holy Spirit came to them in mighty power (Acts 2). The church expanded as God added Gentiles to its numbers. Countless followers of Christ, whose names are no longer known and who traveled because of missionary calling, business, or fleeing persecution, planted churches in major cities all across the Roman Empire.

These new churches preached the gospel of Christ, discipled new converts in the way of obedience, and sought advice from the apostles, whose missionary journeys helped to clarify the practical aspects of living as Christians in the world and with one another. The early church was made up of Jews and Gentiles alike, in unity and love. The church experienced both glorious days, because of God's unique presence in its midst, and difficult days. The political climate was turning increasingly dark for Christians.

Great Commission

"All authority in heaven and on earth has been given to me. Therefore go and make disciples of all nations, baptizing them in the name of the Father and of the Son and of the Holy Spirit, and teaching them to obey everything I have commanded you. And surely I will be with you always, to the very end of the age" (Matt. 28:18–20, NIV).

Peter's Unusual Death

Perhaps the most historically reliable account of an apostle's death is that of Peter, who died during the Neronic persecution. According to several writers of the first and second centuries, Peter was crucified upside-down, refusing in his humility to be killed in the same manner as his Lord.

Nero's Cruelty Toward Christians, A.D. 64

"Nero set up as the culprits and punished with the utmost refinement of cruelty a class hated . . . who are commonly called Christians. . . . [T]hey were clad in the hides of beasts and torn to death by dogs; others were crucified, others set on fire to serve to illuminate the night when daylight failed. Nero had thrown open his grounds for the display, and was putting on a show in the circus, where he mingled with the people in the dress of a charioteer or drove about in his chariot."—Tacitus *Annuals*, xv. 44.

Not long after the Ascension of Christ, many of His followers experienced death at the hands of the Jews or the Roman government. Stephen was stoned by order of the Sanhedrin about the year 35, after which Christians fled to Damascus, beyond the borders of Judea, to Phoenicia, Cyprus, and Antioch (Acts 9; 11). Within just a few years James, the brother of John, was beheaded by Herod Agrippa I in Jerusalem in the year 44 (Acts 12:2). The other James, the brother of Jesus, was put to death in the same city about 62, just prior to the executions of Peter and Paul, which took place in Rome a couple of years later.

Distinctions between Jews and Christians became apparent as Jewish uprisings against Rome surfaced. Christians, who distanced themselves from this growing nationalism, were finally recognized as a separate group from the Jews and were perceived as a threat to the empire on the basis of their numerical growth. Seen as an illegal, heretical sect, Christians were accused of treason and other crimes against the State, even though they were primarily poor and powerless.

They were considered uncompromising and stubborn, even "atheists," refusing to worship visible Roman gods. They were pronounced guilty of licentiousness and immorality, a misrepresentation of the *agape* feasts and the use of phrases like *brothers* and *sisters*. Accused of cannibalism when they partook of the Lord's Supper and haters of humanity when they did not participate in social customs associated with pagan worship, Christians were hunted, off and on, for the next two and a half centuries, beginning with Nero's reign (54–68) and ending with Constantine's (312–37).

These isolated attacks of hatred against the Christians intensified. In the second and part of the third centuries, occasional waves of persecution, like those of Domitian and Marcus Aurelius, swept across areas of the empire. However, although Christianity was illegal, no systematic plan of extermination took place during the 100s. Local authorities and the good will of neighbors primarily determined the fate of most Christians during this period.

In the second century, some Christians took up the task of pleading with the authorities for the legal right to exist. They refuted misconceptions and rumors about their beliefs and practices and made their case for Christianity in a world which defined its realities in philosophical terms. These thinkers and writers were the "apologists," who engaged in warfare of a different kind. Theirs were battles of the mind.

One of the charges leveled against the Christians most difficult to refute was that of intellectual weakness. Christianity was full of contradictions, nonbelievers claimed. The idea of a transcendent, yet immanent God was unreasonable, as was the Jewish-Christian teaching of the resurrection of the body. Some of the roots of such questioning came from the philosophical systems which supported the Hellenistic worldview.

For more than four hundred years the teachings of Socrates and Plato had continued to hold wide appeal and to attract new generations of thinkers. Platonism and its adherence to perfection, found only in the invisible realm, helped to explain many of Christianity's most abstract beliefs.

Ignatius of Antioch

"Now I begin to be a disciple. . . . Let fire and cross, flocks of beasts, broken bones, dismemberment, . . . come upon me, so long as I attain to Jesus Christ"—Pastor of the church at Antioch, who was martyred in Rome about 107.

Agape Feasts

Agape feasts or love feasts were fellowship meals the Christian community celebrated joyfully together with their celebration of the Lord's Supper. For further information on Agape feast, see *Holman Bible Dictionary*, "Love Feast," pp. 898–9.

Christian writers of Justin's day used Platonism and Stoicism to interpret faith to non-Christians. As time went by, however, philosophy began to influence how even Christians understood their own faith.

Justin Martyr is the outstanding Christian apologist of the second century. His writings are considered to be the first of their kind in seeking to reconcile the claims of faith and reason. Eventually scourged and beheaded, his official court death record survives to bear witness to the price he willingly paid to follow Christ. Just as significant are his works, written almost nineteen hundred years ago, which even today challenge believers to engage in an intelligent defense of the Christian faith.

BIOGRAPHICAL BACKGROUND

Almost all that is known about the life of Justin Martyr is found in his own writings. He was born in Flavia Neapolis (modern Nablus), near the ruins of the ancient city of Shechem, close to Jacob's Well, in Syria-Palestine. Flavia Neapolis was named after the Emperor Vespasian (69–79), the ruler who gained control of the empire after Nero's suicide, and it was here that the child Justin was born. His grandfather, Bacchius, whose name is Greek, and his father, Priscus, whose name is Latin, gave to this young son the Latin name, *Justin*, meaning "justice."

By his own account, Justin called himself a Samaritan, although nothing in his writings gives reason to believe that he was familiar with Samaritan customs or religion. His ancestors may have settled in the area soon after Flavia Neapolis was established, about the year 70. For the date of his birth there is little concrete evidence. Much debate centers on the contradictory accounts of his age at the time of his death, somewhere between 162 and 167, during the reign of Marcus Aurelius. He must, therefore, have been born either late in the first century or early in the second.

Justin was raised a Gentile. He said he was uncircumcised, knowing nothing of Moses or the prophets. He received a Greek education and was drawn to the study of philosophy at an early age. In the early chapters of his *Dialogue*, Justin related his youthful journey through the many philosophical schools which abounded in that day. He sat at the feet of several teachers, each of whom gathered around him students eager to learn new ways of thinking about life.

A *Peripatetic* was an itinerant philosopher from the Greek school of Aristotle (382–322 B.C.), one-time student of Plato. The name came from the Greek word, *peripateo*, which means "to walk about," and referred to Aristotle's practice of strolling in the covered Lyceum as he taught. Aristotle was tutor to Alexander the Great and opened a school rivaling that of Plato's Academy in Athens. Aristotle's school specialized in biology, created the science of logic and the theory of causation, and collected a vast library.

JUSTIN'S INTELLECTUAL PILGRIMMAGE

Stoic

↓

Peripatetic

↓

Pythagorean

↓

Platonist

While Justin was studying with his Platonist teacher, he was impressed with the concept of immaterial things, which "gave wings to my mind," he said. Full of this new discovery, Justin went alone one day to the sea to think. There he became a believer in Jesus Christ, through a conversation with a gentle old man, and found the reason for his existence.

Many scholars believe Justin's conversion took place about 130. This was a dramatic turning point in his life. We have little information about the period following Justin's conversion

A *Pythagorean* follows the school of Pythagoras (Born c. 570 B.C.), a philosopher, mathematician, and mystic from Samos, a Greek island off the western coast of Turkey. Pythagoreanism's main beliefs concerned astronomy, the transmigration of the soul (or reincarnation), the concept of "stellar music," and the idea that numbers are the ultimate elements of the universe.

Platonism

Platonism is the study of the teachings of the philosopher Aristocles (427–347 B.C.), known as Plato because of his broad shoulders. Plato, student and defender of Socrates, began a school in Athens, called the Academy, which specialized in mathematics, ethics, and dialogue. Plato developed the Theory of Forms that contrasts the world of sense and everyday experience with a truer and higher, invisible world of ideas.

Conversion in the Sand Dunes

"Straightway a flame was kindled in my soul; and a love of the prophets, and of those men who are friends of Christ, possessed me. . . . I found this philosophy alone to be safe and profitable. Thus, and for this reason, I am a philosopher"—Justin Martyr, *Dialogue*, 8.

and baptism. Historians think he was in Ephesus and Rome for a time, perhaps instructing at various schools, as did other teachers of that day. These traveling teachers, like Valentinus or Lucian, for example, often toured the provinces or lingered for a time in Alexandria or Cyprus, anywhere students would gather to learn. It's probable that Justin would have done the same.

As time went by, Justin's reputation for defending the faith grew. Eusebius wrote, "But Justin was the most noted of those that flourished in those times, who, in the guise of a philosopher, preached the truth of God, and contended for the faith, also, in his writings."[1] Eusebius told of Justin's second visit to Rome and the training sessions that took place in the home of Martinus, who resided over the bath of Timotinus. Several of those who followed Justin to their deaths in later years were part of these groups of early scholar-evangelists who specialized in defending the faith.

One of Justin's pupils was Tatian, a brilliant apologist from Assyria, who authored the first full harmony of the Gospels, called the *Diatesseron*. Scholars think it is possible that Justin's school published a body of literary work upon which later writings, like this harmony, were founded, although no known corpus exists today.

After more than three decades of teaching the truth of God, Justin was denounced as a Christian, along with six of his friends: Chariton, Charito, Euelpistus, Hierax, Paeon, and Liberianus.[2] This denunciation took place at the instigation of a man named Crescens, the cynic philosopher Justin had routed publically in debate. Both *The Acts of the Christian Martyrs* and a surviving official court document recount their deaths. The *Chron Paschale* records that his death took place in the year 165.

They were brought before Rusticus, the prefect of Rome, and were commanded to sacrifice to the gods. Justin refused, replying that "no one who is rightly minded turns from true belief to false." While being interrogated, Justin testified of the truth of Christianity's claims and admitted to holding meetings in the house of Martinus.

After repeatedly refusing to sacrifice, Justin was threatened with death. He answered, "If we are punished for the sake of our Lord Jesus Christ, we hope to be saved." They were then sentenced to scourging with rods and beheading, all of which was quickly carried out. As they died, they praised God, confessing Christ as Savior. Afterwards, friends secretly stole away their bodies for Christian burial.

Justin on Death

"You are able to kill us, but not to hurt us"—Justin Martyr, *First Apology, 2,* addressed to Emperor Marcus Aurelius.

TIME LINE

c. 95?	John the apostle is exiled to Patmos and the book of *Revelation* written. Emperor Domitian (81–96) decrees emperor worship; he also executes or exiles several Christian family members on charges of "atheism"; he is himself murdered.
90–100	Jewish Christians are excluded from synagogue services.
98–117	Trajan becomes emperor, the first ruler to persecute Christians separately from the Jews.
c.100	Justin Martyr is born in Flavia Neapolis (Nablus).
c.100	Rumors begin to circulate that Christians are cannibals.
c.110	Ignatius, pastor of Antioch, is martyred in Rome.
105–6	The Roman Empire reaches its greatest extent following the Dacian (modern Romania) Wars.

TIME LINE

117–38	Emperor Hadrian builds a wall across Britain and secures boundaries of the empire.
118	Population of Rome exceeds one million.
c.125	*Second Clement* is the earliest extant Christian sermon.
c.130	Justin Martyr is converted after conversing with an old man on a beach.
130–65	Justin founds his philosophical schools in Ephesus and Rome and has his dialogue with Trypho the Jew (c.135), which he later publishes under the same name.
132–5	Second Jewish War led by Bar Kokhba.
138–61	Emperor Antoninus Pius takes the throne, to whom Justin later writes his first treatise.
140–60	Heretic Marcion and Gnostic teacher Valentinus are active in Rome; church leaders write against their teachings.
c.155	Polycarp, student of Irenaeus, who was a student of John the Apostle, is martyred.
150–55	Justin Martyr writes his *First Apology*, addressed to Antoninus Pius.
c.155	Justin writes his *Second Apology*, addressed to the Roman Senate.
161–80	When Emperor Marcus Aurelius takes the throne, anti-Christian literature abounds, resulting in horrible executions of Christians, including Justin and his six friends in 165 and the 48 martyrs of Lyons and Vienne in 177.
164	Fifteen-year plague breaks out in the Roman Empire.
165	Justin Martyr and six of his friends are beaten savagely and beheaded.

JUSTIN MARTYR'S THOUGHT

For Justin Martyr, there was no clear distinction between philosophy and theology. These two were combined in the perfect revelation of Jesus Christ; therefore, the best that philosophy offered was but a preparation for the gospel. The treatment and death of Socrates, for example, was a parallel of what was to come in the life of Christ. Just as Socrates tried to bring others to the truth and for his trouble was put to death as an atheist, followers of Christ were convicted on the same charge when bringing His truth to others. In this way, the work of Socrates was an anticipation of Christ's coming and subsequent work (*First Apology,* 5).

On Philosophers. Justin read Christian ideas into Plato. He inferred the doctrine of a personal *logos* from Plato's World-Soul; he held that Moses' teaching in Genesis 1:2 corresponded with Plato's doctrine that God made the world from formless matter and argued that many of Plato's ideas were, in fact, taken from the Old Testament (*First Apology,* 59–60).

The Platonism that Justin held seemed to be a jumble of philosophies and theologies more properly called Middle Platonism. He, along with others like Eudorus of Alexandria (c.25) and Plutarch (b.45), echoed the transitional thinking that linked Platonism and Neoplatonism, the latter of which became the final philosophical achievement of the ancient world.

Barnard has shown that after Justin's lifetime, educated converts no longer felt they had to throw away their previously held philosophical insights but, instead, readily used these as a means to convey theological truth.[3] This shift was not universally regarded as a positive influence, however, as Tertullian soon pointed out in *De Anima,* declaring that Plato was "the sauce (condiment) used by all the heretics."

On the Logos. Another contribution to the philosophy and theology of his day was Justin's

Philosophy in Scripture

The only place the word "philosophy" is used in the biblical text is in Colossians 2:8 (NIV): "See to it that no one takes you captive through hollow and deceptive philosophy, which depends on human tradition and the basic principles of this world rather than on Christ."

Stoicism

Stoicism, slightly younger than Platonism, held strongly to the laws of nature and humankind's duty to obey and adjust to them. One of the natural laws is reason, Stoics claimed, and wisdom consists in subduing the extremes of human passion to universal reason so that one is left with the four virtues: moral insight, courage, self-control, and justice.

No Easy Discovery

"It is neither easy to find the Father and Maker of all, nor, having found Him is it safe to declare Him to all."—Justin Martyr, *Second Apology,* 10, quoting *Timaeus,* Plato's theory of physics.

unique use and application of the term "*logos spermatikos,*" or "germinative" Word. The term *logos* was well known in Stoic circles, as it was in Jewish and Christian theology. Yet with Justin's new definition, Christianity became as old as Creation. Whatever was good or true in the writings of the pagans derived from the logos in them. This argument was aimed at the philosophers who had claimed that Christianity was merely borrowing from their sources.

For Justin, only in Jesus Christ could the entirety of the *logos* be found. The eternal Christ, however, was "sowing the seeds" of Himself in people throughout history, like the Gospel parable of the sower. As the seeds of truth were sown in their hearts and individuals conformed themselves to that truth, they reaped a harvest of right living and right knowledge, a bounty of religious and moral illumination (*Second Apology* 6, 8, 10, 13). This explains, according to Justin, why there were Christians before Christ and how active and divine potential existed in humankind before the time of Jesus.[4] This is considered by scholars to be exceptionally original thought.

On the Trinity. All things considered, however, Justin was not a systematic theologian as such. His doctrinal views must be pieced from his writings. His concept of God was monotheistic, grounded in the religion of Israel. Still, after his conversion, it was somewhat Platonistic, with God as transcendent and unknowable. God was the Unmoved First Cause, distant and unreachable, who worked solely through the *logos* to communicate with humankind (*Dialogue,* 127).

Justin expounded no clear doctrine of the Trinity in his Apologies. Although each person of the Trinity is worthy of worship, he seems to have written no clear exposition of the relationship between each person of the Godhead. His theology, rather, seems to have been born out of Christian experience and worship in the church. He spoke of the Spirit, who inspired prophets and gives gifts to the church and the guide of all spiritual work. He spoke of the Son, the *logos*, divine bridge between God and human beings. He spoke of the Father, supreme in the Universe (*First Apology, 13, 61, 63, 65, 67; and Second Apology, 6*). His terms for the Trinity are traditional formulas; demonstrating, perhaps, how church life impacted his language and thought here more than any other influence.

On the Church and Sacraments. Justin believed himself to be a traditionalist in his view of ecclesiology. Staunchly avowing that the church had been founded by the Apostles in the name of Christ, church doctrine and polity, like Communion and baptism rites, followed the pattern he believed had been faithfully handed down. His explanations of these rites are fully developed and are the most complete to survive from the second century.

Baptism, Justin believed, should take place only after a period of thorough discipleship and preparation. By his accounts, it seems the church was holding annual baptismal services, perhaps at Easter, when those newly baptized could celebrate the entire gospel story in its fullest. As the candidate was washed three times in water, at each washing the name of each person of the Trinity was spoken over him. Baptism took place in the name of the Trinity; and a confession, perhaps of Christ's death and belief in

The Logos

The Greek term, *logos*, is used by John in the prologue of his Gospel. Here Christ is the divine expression of God—God's speech, mode of communication, the "Word of the Lord" in the Old Testament, and the use of "word" for the gospel in the New Testament. John may also have had in mind the personification of wisdom in Jewish thought, the surrogate term for God in the Targums, and the Reason which governs the universe, which the Stoics and Philo understood. Yet John here boldly dared to combine God and the historical person of Jesus into the same term—the *Logos*.

Luke 12:4–5

"I tell you, my friends, do not be afraid of those who kill the body and after that can do no more. But I will show you whom you should fear: Fear him who, after the killing of the body, has power to throw you into hell. Yes, I tell you, fear him" (Luke 12:4–5, NIV). Justin's view of death demonstrates both biblical understanding and knowledge of the Stoics, who also believed that external evil could not hurt a truly righteous person.

the Trinitarian nature of the Godhead, was made (*First Apology,* 61, 65).

Baptism also signified new birth. Justin quoted John 3:3: "I tell you the truth, no one can see the kingdom of God unless he is born again" (NIV), and made a point to connect illumination of the *logos* with baptism (*First Apology,* 61). For Justin, the candidate is enabled to live an obedient, moral life at the point of baptism which, if he or she is careful to make a true home for the resident Spirit of God, will result in increasing godliness. Right living, then, is the real measure of faith.

Likewise, the Lord's Supper, or Eucharist, as Justin called it, was celebrated at two occasions in the life of the church. The first was following baptism, in the presence of the church and the witnesses, when the newly baptized received for the first time the wine and water and the bread. A prayer was said for the new members and Christians all over the world, followed by a kiss of peace. As each candidate received the elements, he or she offered praise to the Father of the universe through the name of the Son and the Holy Spirit. This was followed by the candidate's public thanksgiving, after which the congregation joined in with a joyous *amen.*

The other practice of the Eucharist celebration in the church took place each Sunday morning during worship. At these times, the people heard a portion of Scripture read, followed by an exposition of the text, and then the congregation prayed while standing. Then the deacons brought the elements to the "Ruler," who offered a prayer and thanksgiving. The wine and bread were then given to those present. Finally, a voluntary offering was taken for those in need (orphans, widows, sick, visitors), to be distributed by the Ruler. Justin interestingly noted that in both of the Communion services the deacons took the elements to those who were absent, the earliest reference to this practice (*First Apology*, 65–67).

In Justin's thought, Christ was present in the wine and wafer. Through further action of the *logos*, the elements become united with the *logos* and thereby becomes the flesh and blood of the Incarnate Jesus. By the use of an analogy, Justin questioned why it is difficult to understand this spiritual transformation that takes place in the Eucharist when the body's natural process of food digestion results in the production of actual flesh and blood (*First Apology*, 66).

On Demons. On a somewhat darker and final note, one of Justin's underlying theological presuppositions, his view of the demonic, should perhaps be addressed. Like his contemporaries in Greek philosophical and Jewish circles, Justin believed in the existence of fallen angels, who had sinned with women and produced demon children. These demons, in turn, had propagated a whole race of evil warriors upon the earth, whose goal it was to win control of the universe through the souls of men and women. Their activity could be readily demonstrated.

They were responsible for leading astray pagan poets and mythologists who mistook them for gods, for perverting Christian ordinances into pagan temple worship and purification rites, for instigating the injury of anyone responding to the *logos* in times past, and especially for persecuting the Christians of his day (*First Apology*, 62). In Justin's thought, Christians could exercise control over these evil ones through the rite

Demons Pervert the Truth

"From what has been said you can understand how the demons, in imitation of what was said through Moses, contrived also to raise up the image of the so-called Kore over the springs of the waters saying that she was a daughter of Zeus. For Moses said, as he wrote before: 'In the beginning God made the heaven and the earth. And the earth was invisible and unfurnished, and the Spirit of God moved over the waters.' In imitation, then, of what is said of the Spirit of God moving on the water they spoke of Kore, daughter of Zeus"—Justin Martyr, *First Apology*, 64.

of exorcism, which in itself was symbolic of the final victory of the Second Coming of Christ (*Second Apology,* 5). As Justin defended his faith to the Greek world, these beliefs both helped to define his thought and motivated his zeal for ultimate triumph.

WRITINGS ATTRIBUTED TO HIM

Justin Martyr's works are considered to be among the most important of the materials which have survived from the second century. These may be classified into three categories: those which are undisputedly his, those whose authorship has been debated, and those which claim to be his but are unquestionably not.

The first grouping includes just three works. Justin authored two volumes entitled *Apology*. Some scholars believe that there may have been at one time three such books or portions of books. Eusebius spoke of two volumes, one written in the reign of Antoninus Pius, and one written under Marcus Aurelius. Perhaps what is now considered to be *First Apology* and *Second Apology* were once one volume, and the original second volume has been lost. Perhaps Eusebius made a mistake in his citation of which emperor was in power at the time of writing.

At any rate, the first source constitutes the bulk of what is known about how Christians and non-Christians related to each other in those days. It also attempts, for the first time, to reconcile the claims of faith and reason. The second volume primarily defends specific charges against Christians.

The third book in the category is called *Dialogue with Trypho the Jew*, the first detailed exposition of why Christ should be considered to be the Messiah of the Old Testament. It also exposes the changing nature of the Old Covenant and its laws; it identifies the *logos* with the God of the Old Testament; and it sets forth the argument that Gentiles (here, Christians) are the true heirs of God's promises to Israel.

The second grouping of books, whose authorship is still sometimes debated, consists of *An Address to the Greeks*, *A Hortatory Address to the Greeks*, *On the Monarchy of God*, *An Epistle to Diognetus*, fragments from a work on the Resurrection, and other fragments. Most scholars feel that these all date from the late second and third centuries and are spurious.

The final category of writings that bore his name has also proven to be false. These Pseudo-Justinian works, including *An Exposition of the True Faith*, *Replies to the Orthodox*, *Christian Questions to Gentiles*, *Gentile Questions to Christians*, *Epistle to Zenas and Serenus*, and *A Refutation of Certain Doctrines of Aristotle*, seem to be from a single author from the fourth- or fifth-century Aristotelian school.

An examination of Justin Martyr's three most important works will now follow. Attention will be given to each volume in turn, beginning with a look at date, purpose, and audience, followed by a summary and notes on each section. The first volume will be Justin's *First Apology*.

FIRST APOLOGY   - - - -

"So you, then, since you are called pious and philosophers and guardians of justice and lovers of culture, listen in every way; and it will be shown if you are such" (ch. 2).

DATE, PURPOSE, AND AUDIENCE

The dating of the Apologies is one of the intriguing aspects of Justin Martyr studies. Unless further information comes to light, this puzzle may remain a mystery. The first volume, addressed to the "Emperor Titus Aelius Adrianus Antoninus Pius, Augustus Caesar; and to his son Verissimus the philosopher, and to Lucius the philosopher" is plainly intended for Emperor Antoninus and his two sons. Antoninus followed Hadrian to the Roman throne in 138 and reigned until 161, when his son Marcus Aurelius succeeded him.

The *First Apology* also contains a reference to Marcionism, a Gnostic sect, as the greatest heresy of the age. Historians place Marcion in Rome during the reign of Hyginus, between 139 and 142. These and other internal data suggest that the years 151 to 155 would be a correct period for the publication of this timely document. The more problematic dating of the second volume will be taken up in the next chapter.

The purpose of the *First Apology* is clearly defined as well. The first salvo strikes an appeal for justice and follows quickly with a refutation of anti-Christian slander. Justin's intentions are indisputable. His first aim was to win from the government of Rome a hearing—ultimately, the right for Christianity to exist as a coherent, logical, reasonable, and legal religion. Second, Justin explained the Christian faith, its teachings, practices, and rationale to the Greek world.

The audience of *First Apology* is urbane, cosmopolitan, intelligent, and powerful. His intended readers are despots, whose whims determine the fate of individuals without guarantee of a fair hearing. Justin knew that his life hung in the

Marcion

Marcion was a wealthy shipowner from the region of Pontus. He came to Rome around A.D. 140 and became a part of the Christian church. Marcion was excommunicated around 144. He rejected the Old Testament and viewed the God of the Old Testament, the Demiurge, as inferior to the God revealed in Jesus Christ. Marcion accepted as Scripture ten letters of Paul, excluding Hebrews and 1, 2 Timothy and Titus. He further edited even these writings he accepted as Scripture.

balance, that he had cast his lot with a despised people. His writings, while not known for their polish or style, do resound with heroic pleadings and undaunted courage.

FIRST APOLOGY AT A GLANCE

Chapters 1–2	Salutations and an Appeal for Justice
Chapters 3–12	Refutation of Anti-Christian Slanders
Chapter 13	Christian Worship
Chapters 14–20	Christian Teaching Versus Nature and Philosophy
Chapters 21–22	Pagan Fables Versus Rational Belief in Christ
Chapter 23	Divinity of Christ Explained
Chapters 24–29	Intolerance of Impostors Implored
Chapters 30–53	Proofs of Prophecy Fulfilled
Chapters 54–58	Mythology and Christ
Chapters 59–60	Plato, Moses, and the Creation Story
Chapters 61–67	Christian Baptism and Communion
Chapter 68	Conclusion

Justin's Opinion of a Heretic

"The wicked demons have put forward Marcion of Pontus, who is even now teaching people to deny that God is the Maker of all things in heaven and earth, and that the Christ predicted through his prophets is His Son, and proclaims another god besides the Demiurge of all and likewise another son. Many are persuaded by him as if he alone knew the truth, and laugh at us, though they have no proof of the things they say, but are snatched away irrationally as lambs by a wolf, and become the prey of godless teaching and of demons" (ch. 58).

CHAPTERS 1–2: SALUTATIONS AND AN APPEAL FOR JUSTICE

The opening paragraph of *First Apology* contains Justin Martyr's address to the Emperor Antoninus Pius, Augustus Caesar, and his two sons. Justin referred to the boys as "philosophers," a term often used for young children. He also saluted the "Sacred Senate" and the Roman

Roman Senate

Composed of 300 of the true aristocracy, the Roman Senators held their seats for life, unless proven to have been dishonorable. The decisions of the Senate were made on behalf of the people of Rome. Justin's salutation, then, recognized this aspect of the Senate's vast power.

Justice Demanded

"Reason dictates that those who are truly pious and philosophical should honor and love only the truth, declining to follow the opinions of the ancients, if they are worthless. . . . But it is for you, as reason demands, to listen [to us] and to be found good judges. For if, having learned the truth, you fail to do what is righteous, you have no defense before God" (ch. 2–3).

people on behalf of those of every nation who are "unjustly hated and grossly abused, . . . myself being one of them." He then simply signed his name Justin, son of Priscus and grandson of Bacchius, from Flavia Neapolis in Syria-Palestine.

Chapter 2 lays the foundation for Justin's plea for understanding. He appealed first to those who love truth and honor, on the basis of reason and piety, to render decisions based on a fair hearing. He denounced those who would judge according to superstition, flattery, prejudice, irrational impulse, or evil rumors. If his hearers are guardians of justice and lovers of culture, then listen accordingly, he said, and the outcome will prove what kind of men they really are.

CHAPTERS 3–12: REFUTATION OF ANTI-CHRISTIAN SLANDERS

The request for investigation follows in chapter 3. Justin logically stated that if, after the inquiry is finished, the charges have been proved to be true, then the Christians should be punished according to their crimes. If not, he cautioned, reason forbids wronging innocent people. He quoted Plato, who said: "Unless both rulers and the ruled love wisdom, it is impossible to make cities prosper" (ch. 3).

Justin took exception to the practice of punishing Christians merely for bearing that name. He argued that if someone denies he is a Christian he is then set free because no evil has been found in him. On the other hand, if someone claims the name of Christ, then he is punished, whether his life is blameless or sinful. Justin challenged his listeners to inquire into the life of both and let the life of each determine his own fate. He acknowledged that in Christianity, just as in philosophy, there are those who live counterfeit to the faith they claim. Therefore, each person should be judged individually according to his deeds.

In chapter 5, Justin explained how demons corrupt men and women, strike fear into them, and delude their understanding. This is what happens when men are ruled by passion rather than reason. Justin expressed concern that those to whom he was appealing would recognize the demonic influence lurking behind their unjust judgment of Christians.

These demons, whose leader is Satan, were proclaimed gods; and all evil is ascribed to their agency. Then Socrates, through reason and evidence, sought to help illuminate the people to see the truth but was charged as an atheist and killed for his noble teaching. *Logos* revealed this truth not only to the Greeks through Socrates but to foreigners and others as well.

In chapters 6–8, Justin answered the specific charges of atheism, immorality, and disloyalty. He admitted that Christians are atheists with reference to the pantheon of deities. But as for the one true God, He is worshiped and adored, together with his Son "who came from Him, and taught us these things," (ch. 6) and the prophetic Spirit, to whom is given honor in reason and truth.

He confessed that Christians do not honor with sacrifices and garlands of flowers the deities people have made and set in the temples. He thought it preposterous that artisans ply their trades in the fashioning of temple idols by their "planning and cutting, casting, and hammering" (ch. 9). No one even questions, he said, the

Carpocracians

Justin was aware, no doubt, of the sect known as Carpocracians (a group sometimes confused with the Egyptian cult of Harpocrates). The followers of Carpocrates of Alexandria preached a license to sin, or antinomianism. This teaching suggests, however wrongly, that Christians are by grace set free from the need to observe any moral law; therefore, sin is no longer accounted to the individual. He also taught the transmigration of souls (reincarnation) and that Jesus was born of natural birth. This sect survived until the fourth century.

notion that God cannot be copied or shaped by the hands of man: "What stupidity, that dissolute people should be said to fashion and make gods for public worship, and that you should appoint such people the guardians of temples, . . . not recognizing that it is unlawful even to think or say that people are the guardians of gods" (ch. 9).

Instead, chapter 10 explains, God does not need material possessions. Indeed, He alone is the giver of all things. God is the one who created everything out of unformed matter. If human beings choose what is pleasing to Him and align their lives to His design, then they become worthy to reign with Him. God both persuades and leads people to faith by means of the rational powers He gives freely and by the *Logos*. Justin observed that there is something within human beings—the lust of wickedness—which resists the work of the *Logos* and the exercise of reason. This lust of wickedness is encouraged and strengthened by demons.

Chapter 11 carefully defines what kingdom Christians seek. Others had charged that Christians look for another kingdom, perhaps fearing that they would disturb the *Pax Romana*. Justin revealed his deep respect for Christian martyrs when he said that the kingdom Christians seek is one with God. If they wanted to overthrow the government, they would hide their allegiance and try to escape detection. But since they do not seek a human kingdom, Christians willingly testify to their faith, even though they know such a confession will bring death.

The final chapter in this section assures his hearers that Christians are proponents of peace. They live openly under the sight of God, know-

Justin's appeal here has parallel with Paul's apology on Mars' Hill: "Ye men of Athens, I perceive that in all things ye are too superstitious. For as I passed by, and beheld your devotions, I found an altar with this inscription, TO THE UNKNOWN GOD. Whom therefore ye ignorantly worship, him declare I unto you. God that made the world and all things therein, seeing that he is Lord of heaven and earth, dwelleth not in temples made with hands; Neither is worshipped with men's hands, as though he needed any thing" (Acts 17:22–25, KJV).

ing that it is impossible for "the wicked, the covetous, the conspirator, and the virtuous" (ch. 12) to escape God's notice. If all persons understood this, Justin asserted, then no one would choose wickedness even for a little while. Eternal destiny is determined by character, and this is demonstrated by how one lives. With tongue in cheek Justin suggested, "But you seem to fear lest all people become righteous, and you no longer have any to punish. This would be the concern of public executioners, not of good princes" (ch. 12). He concluded by restating that God will bring about the prophecies foretold and that all things given and taught by Jesus Christ are indeed true and may be trusted.

My Kingdom Is Not Your Kingdom

"Jesus said, 'My kingdom is not of this world. If it were, my servants would fight to prevent my arrest by the Jews. But now my kingdom is from another place.'
'You are a king, then!' said Pilate.
Jesus answered, 'You are right in saying I am a king. In fact, for this reason I was born, and for this I came into the world, to testify to the truth. Everyone on the side of truth listens to me'" (John 18:36–37, NIV).

 ## COMMENTARY

Plea for a Fair Hearing. In these first two major divisions, readers are introduced to the remarkably courageous Justin Martyr. Although many Christians in Rome and other cities may have known him, there are no extant sources to suggest that the Roman authorities knew him personally. Therefore, when Justin took up his pen to write these words, he consciously chose to place his life in jeopardy and to suffer whatever consequences such an action might bring. It is the decision to move away from the crowd in the shadows, to step into the spotlight alone, to become public defender.

The details of Justin Martyr's life are few. No sources indicate whether Justin had a wife or children. Nothing is written of his mother, siblings, or extended family. Of his particular interests and hobbies, the serendipities of life that delighted his soul, nothing is recorded. What is

Reputation for Faithfulness

Sometimes we Christians live with tunnel vision, not remembering that so many faithful ones have gone before us or that we are like links in a chain for those who will come after. Each of us has but one life with which to serve God. When this life has gone, others will fill the pages of the kingdom's history. Now is the time to impact eternity. You are the player on this stage today. How you decide to obey God, or to reject Him, will determine how kingdom history is recorded. God can impact eternity with just one life totally yielded to Him. Will those who come behind you write of your faithfulness?

known is this: He was born; he trained in philosophy; and he was converted. He taught for some twenty-five years that the gospel was the only way to salvation and that Christianity was the one completely valid philosophy. He was brutally murdered for refusing to sacrifice to idols. He was buried in an unknown place by those who loved him.

What would cause a man of Justin's obvious talent and training to choose this journey for himself? The opening statements of *First Apology* answer this question without hesitation. These bold declarations reveal his passion, his uncompromising stance, even his "in your face" contempt of danger. Readers snatch a glimpse, for the first time, of Justin Martyr's mind at work. One wonders what reactions raced across the faces of the senators and authorities who first read the treatise. That Justin aligned himself with the "unjustly hated and grossly abused" (ch. 1) shoots to the heart of his illustrious audience. There is no mistaking with whom he stands.

Next on Justin's agenda was to present a clear argument for intentional justice, which he did in appealing to reason and truth. After all, he asked, are these not the foundations of anyone who claims to be pious and a lover of all that is righteous (both true goals of philosophy)? What follows is a cataloguing of the rumors and slanders of which Christians have been accused, and evidence is given for their dismissal. He seems to have prioritized the lies according to their severity and almost dismissed as misunderstandings the more simple of the list. The severe charges he dealt with separately: atheism, immorality, and treason. These touch upon theological issues, and so he used this window of opportunity to teach his readers about what true Christians believe.

Worshiping the one, true God alone was interpreted by the Roman authorities as atheism. Justin redefined for them the terms *god* and *atheist* here, saving a discussion about what constitutes true worship for the following chapter. He introduced his readers to the only God, the Father of righteousness, His Son and Holy Spirit, and offered freely the transforming gospel message to any who would hear.

He addressed the serious charge of immorality because righteous living is, for Justin, the mark of true faith. Nonbelievers were pointing to the wickedness of those who claimed to be Christians as evidence that Christianity was false. Justin took great exception to this charge. He rightly stated that in any faith or philosophical system there are those who claim the name but whose lives fall short of the standard. A person who claims to be a believer but whose life does not bear out the claims of Christ, however, does not invalidate Christianity, Justin argued, anymore than does the ignorance of those who merely claim to be philosophers invalidate the given philosophical system. Modern readers identify well with this point.

It is always troublesome when people claiming to belong to Christ break the law, exist for self, and pervert the truth. Nonbelievers will accept no testimony of Christ's transforming power from a corrupt witness. This is only right. Justin shut the argument down when he shifted the focus from defining a person not by what he *says*, but by *who* he *is* revealed in what he *does*. Justin reasonably asserted that action defines character, not mere words. True Christians will

Two Lists of the Faithful

In Hebrews 11, known as the Faith chapter, God commends two lists—the recitation of those recognized names of the Old Testament faithful and the many whose names are unrecorded who suffered for their faith: "Others were tortured and refused to be released, so that they might gain a better resurrection. Some faced jeers and flogging, while still others were chained and put in prison. They were stoned; they were sawed in two; they were put to death by the sword. They went about in sheepskins and goatskins, destitute, persecuted and mistreated—the world was not worthy of them" (Heb. 11:35–38, NIV).

be identified by their obedient lives. This is a message the church needs to hear today.

The charge of disloyalty, or treason, was also in need of redefinition. Christians were some of the best citizens of the Roman Empire, Justin noted. Lovers of peace, seekers of truth, finders of genuine faith, Christians lived under the watchful eyes of God, as did the rest of the realm. The kingdom of Christ was a spiritual domain, not a human kingdom. Here Justin's respect for the martyrs shines in his statements about the Christians' fearlessness in the face of death. Justin challenged the authorities to do what they felt was needful but warned them that they would not ultimately succeed.

"If we looked for a human kingdom, we would deny it, that we might not be slain; and we would try to escape detection, that we might obtain the things we look for. But since we do not have our hope on the present, we do not heed our executioners" (ch. 11).

CHAPTER 13: CHRISTIAN WORSHIP

Justin began the second major section of his *First Apology* by presenting how Christians live and what they believe to be true. The opening section, chapter 13, tells his readers that Christians worship the one, true God, who is the Maker of all things. This God does not desire burned offerings, blood, poured wine, or other forms of worship common to the Roman Empire. Instead, Christians believe that God desires hearts of thankfulness expressed in prayer and hymns and testimony. Believers thank Him for creation, for health, for the changing seasons, and answered prayer. Christians look to a future with God beyond this world—beyond corruption. Faith in Christ is the door to this future.

"Our teacher of these things is Jesus Christ, who was also born for this purpose, and was crucified under Pontius Pilate, procurator of Judaea, in the time of Tiberius Caesar; and . . . that we worship Him rationally, having learned that He is the Son of the true God Himself, and holding Him in the second place, and the prophetic Spirit in the third" (ch. 13).

 COMMENTARY

Christian Worship. Justin said that if reasonable men will look at the behavior of Christians they will conclude that they aren't atheists but worship the living God, Maker of the universe.

CHAPTERS 14–20: CHRIST'S TEACHING VERSES NATURE AND PHILOSOPHY

Chapters 14–20 explain the power Christians have for moral victory. This takes place in spite of the efforts of evil ones who strive to conquer human beings. These demons, Justin said, through dreams or magical arts, seek to subdue all who have not claimed the power of Christ and His Word. Justin invited his readers to see the specific ways that Christ has transformed the believers:

- those who formerly delighted in sexual debauchery were now chaste;
- those who practiced sorcery now dedicated themselves wholly to the "good and unbegotten God" (ch. 14);
- those who once valued above all else the gaining of wealth and possessions now take joy in sharing and in giving away to those in need;
- those who once hated and destroyed one another and would not share the same hearth with people of a different race, background, or customs now live "familiarly with them, and pray for our enemies" (ch. 14), so that they, too, might come to know Christ.

Justin then related the reason believers live so differently now. The teachings of Jesus, who was "no sophist" but whose "word was the power of God" (ch. 14), guides His followers into new ways of thinking and acting. Justin recounted some of these teachings, beginning in chapter 15.

Madness of Christians

"For they charge our madness to consist in this, that we give to a crucified man second place after the unchangeable and eternal God, begetter of all things, for they do not know the mystery involved in this, to which we ask you to give heed as we expound it to you" (ch. 13).

On chastity, Justin cited several of Jesus' remarks about sexual behavior, promiscuity, and divorce and remarriage, beginning with Matthew 5:28; that "whosoever looks upon a woman to lust after her has already committed adultery with her in his heart" (ch. 15). Justin added "before God" to the end of this phrase, perhaps trying to remind his pagan readers that God sees all. He followed up with Matthew 5:29–30; Matthew 18:9; Mark 9:47; Luke 16:18; and Matthew 19:11–12.

Justin then gave a personal witness of knowing many men and women, "who have been Christ's disciples from childhood, have preserved their purity at the age of sixty or seventy years; and I am proud that I could produce such from every race of men and women." What is to account for this turning from intemperance to righteousness, asked Justin?

Better yet, what is to account for the affection Christians have for others? Believers pray for enemies, bless those that curse them, share with the needy, lend without thought of return, and lay up treasure in heaven instead of on earth. They are kind and merciful; do not worry about daily provisions, since they know that the Father will supply their needs; and do good deeds out of simple love of God, not to be seen of men. Justin cited Sermon on the Mount passages that teach these truths.

Concerning patience, servant-heartedness, and the love of peace, Justin quoted Christ's teachings on offering the other cheek to those that smite, giving the cloak as well as the shirt to those that ask, and traveling two miles when just one is required. Believers should not quarrel; neither should they imitate wicked people;

they should never swear or speak deceitfully; they should fulfill the first commandment to "worship the Lord your God and Him only shall you serve with all your heart and all your strength, the Lord who made you" (ch. 16).

He reminded his readers that not every one who confesses to be a Christian is truly of Christ, for believers' lives must bear testimony of His transforming power. Justin quoted several verses to justify these last two positions: Matthew 7:15–19, 22–24; 10:40; 24:5; Luke 6:46ff; 10:16; 13:26–27; 21:8; and Mark 13:6. All word pictures, the passages teach believers to go beyond what is asked in order to demonstrate gentle-heartedness. They also warn that not all persons will belong to Christ in eternity. It was important for Justin's readers to understand the motives that propelled believers to action or reaction in their daily lives.

In chapter 17 Justin explained why, when Christians worship God alone, they still faithfully pay their taxes and assessments when levied. He cited the time Jesus answered the question of allegiance by replying, "Give therefore to Caesar the things that are Caesar's, and to God the things that are God's" (Matt. 22:15–22). He assured the Roman authorities that believers gladly serve them in all other aspects besides worship, even praying that their imperial power will eventuate in sound judgment.

If, however, they chose not to regard the prayers of believers, he told them, then it did not matter. Justin explained that every person will give account for his or her actions according to the abilities that were given by God: "To whom God has given more, from him more will be

Good Works Shine

"You are the light of the world. A city on a hill cannot be hidden. Neither do people light a lamp and put it under a bowl. Instead they put it on its stand, and it gives light to everyone in the house. In the same way, let your light shine before men, that they may see your good deeds and praise your Father in heaven" (Matt. 5:14–16, NIV).

Innocent Victims

The writings of Cicero's *Oration in Vatinium*, Socrates's *Ecclesiastical History*, Eusebius's *Ecclesiastical History*, and *Pseudo-Clementine Recognitions* all suggest that children were sometimes taken prematurely from the womb and slaughtered and their entrails inspected for omens of the future.[5]

required" (Luke 12:48) (ch. 17). This will happen after life, as it is now known, has ended.

Chapter 18 speaks to this life after death. Justin demonstrated ways his contemporaries accepted that consciousness from "beyond the grave" existed. These examples were in their own literature. He cited necromancy, or "oracles of the dead," claiming to foretell the future by allegedly communicating with the dead; divinations practiced through innocent children; and the "invoking of departed . . . souls, . . . magi, dream-senders and familiars."

Justin cited those who were "seized and torn by the spirits of the dead" and the oracles of Amphilocus, Dodona, Pytho, and many others (ch. 18). He rolled through the litany of authors whose works told of this consciousness: Empedocles, Pythagoras, Plato, and Socrates, even Homer's *Inferno* and the descent of Odysseus. Justin argued that Christians believe in the one true God more than all of these. Why should his readers scoff at the Christian belief of life after death? Believers should be heard, therefore, and their teachings accorded at least as much credence as were the beliefs of these authors and cults.

Chapter 19 is a case for the certainty of Christian resurrection. The logical problems associated with the bodily and incorruptible resurrection of believers had caused pagans to scoff at Christianity. Justin Martyr postulated that this idea is not at all illogical. His argument was that it is just as impossible to conceive of a full-grown human being when first confronted with the human "seed," as it is to think that a person may rise again when his body has "dis-

The Roman Empire's "Familiar Spirits"

In Justin Martyr's day, most people believed in survival after death. They also believed that one could communicate with the departed; and many employed conjurors, or "contact persons," who specialized in such trade. The *Oneiropompoi* is a term used generally for spirits who operated through dreams. The *Paredroi* were spirits sent to watch over particular persons to keep them from harm—hence, "familiar." The Bible warns against associations of these kind: "The cowardly, the unbelieving, the vile, the murderers, the sexually immoral, those who practice magic arts, the idolaters and all liars—their place will be in the fiery lake of burning sulfur" (Rev. 21:8, NIV).

solved" in the grave. One would think both to be entirely contrary to reason.

Yet human beings do grow from the seed of two parents. Just because his readers had never seen a dead man rise again does not mean that it is not possible, Justin said. To say that resurrection is impossible says more about their concept of God than it does about them. Justin said that believers do better to "believe things impossible to our own nature and to men and women, than to disbelieve like the rest of the world" (ch. 19).

Once again, Justin argued from contemporary literature and philosophy that a final destruction was imminent. Sibyl and Hystaspes both mentioned a destruction by fire of corruptible things, as did the Stoics, who believed that the world and God Himself would be destroyed by fire, only to be reborn into a new form.

Why are Christians silenced, when they claim some of the same things as philosophers and poets, whom his readers honor? Justin asked. If believers state that all things have been ordered and made by God, they sound much like Plato; when they say that the world will be destroyed by fire, they appear to be like Stoics. Christians, who have many similar beliefs, even adding points of clarification and proof beyond the poets and philosophers, should not be unjustly hated but be accorded the same tolerance, even State protection, as do these other belief systems (ch. 20).

Oracles and Grove Worship

Amphilocus was the son of Amphiarus, whose oracle was located at Mallos in Cilicia and mentioned by Pausanias about 180. Dodona was the oracle of Zeus that operated in the groves of oak and beech and Pytho was the famous oracle of Apollo at Delphi. Oracles, in Greek and Roman culture, were places where deities were consulted. Often small temples or altars were erected near a stream, on a mountaintop, or in a grove, where people came to worship or offer sacrifices of blood or libation, or to burn incense to the deity. The word was also used for a person who was believed to be the agency of communication with the god.

 COMMENTARY

Faith and Life of Christians. In the section above, Justin began a careful exposition of what motivates Christians toward righteous living. Such a view begins with a statement about who God is. This is always the best place to start. Christians have their being in and through God, who is the Giver and Maker of all things. Therefore, a right response to Him is adoration and worship, hymn singing and spoken witness to His greatness and mercy.

Thereafter, Justin concerned himself with the practical application of the teachings of Christ. He systematically covered the topics of transformed lives in the areas of chastity, of returning good for evil, of giving to the needy, of showing mercy, of trusting God's provision. He showed how Christians live out patient, servant-hearted, and gentle lives; how Christians pay their taxes and pray for their government.

Some scholars believe that Justin may have used at least one harmony when he wrote this section of his *Apology*. This source, perhaps many such sources, are not now extant but may have been widely available to other church fathers, upon which works their writings seem to be similarly based.[6] During the time Justin taught in Rome, it seems he wrote catechisms for his students, manuals of instruction against heresies, and harmonies of the synoptic Gospel texts.

Justin's source quotations are generally based on the Sermon on the Mount, with additional related material from other parts of Matthew, Mark, and Luke. Justin seems to have used little or no direct quotations from John's work. While no organic link has been proven to have existed between the two schools, other works like these were used in the Alexandrian school some years after Justin's death. Clement and Origen, both of Alexandria, Irenaeus of Lyons, and the

Pseudo-Clementine *Homilies* all depended on a literary tradition which Justin also used.

So it may be safe to surmise that some of these catechisms and church manuals were written by Justin and his pupils there in Rome for the purpose of teaching the faith to new converts. One of Justin's most famous pupils, Tatian, was also an apologist. His *Diatessaron* is the first known complete harmony of the four Gospels, including that of John. Tatian must have enjoyed his study of a selection of limited harmonies; after Justin's death he published his new work.

There is much to be said for a simple catechism in church life. Many evangelical traditions incorporate a period of catechism for new converts. In the early church, those preparing for Christian baptism underwent an often lengthy period of training. They attended services of Bible reading and theological instruction. They learned early on in their journey of faith how the church worshiped, how Christians lived, and what was expected of believers. After this process, the "catechumen" would become a regular participant in church life.

Twenty-first century Christians need the same training in Christian discipleship as did their brothers and sisters of the first and second centuries. Churches need to take precautions that church membership is not based upon a mere verbal "statement," "transfer of letter," or request for membership alone. How churches view new converts says volumes about their view of the church and, ultimately, the kingdom of God. It reveals what they believe about God Himself. Of what sort of persons is the church to consist? The New Testament is clear that the

A Harmony of Scripture

A harmony is a specific genre of literature that arranges parallel passages of different authors so as to bring out corresponding ideas, qualities, and nuances of meaning. In Justin's limited harmony, he used Matthew, Mark, and Luke, but not the Gospel of John. The first three Gospels are called "synoptic Gospels," as distinguished from the fourth, because they present the life of Christ from a similar point of view.

church is made up of those who are redeemed in Christ.

Jesus' kingdom principles run counter to every formula for worldly success. How does one get ahead in business? How does one respond when wronged? How does one get rich in this life? How does one best spend time, money, talents? How does one prepare for the future? How does one deal with sorrow? unfair treatment? others who are difficult to live with? those whose aim is to inflict harm?

Is "evangelism" perhaps so difficult these days because the world sees such little evidence of victorious, deeply satisfying, and joyous life in Christ? Would we truly need all the programs, training, special events, and outreach efforts if, in fact, lives in the church were powerfully transformed?

These dynamic principles, made real in the life of the believer through the illumination of the Holy Spirit, cause followers of Christ to respond oppositely to expectations of the world. When Christians react to the day-in-day-out difficulties of life according to the teachings of their Savior, the world stops to take notice.

Justin's arguments for Christian living, the result of the transforming power of God in and through the life of the believer, is a powerful reminder to, and indictment on, today's church. Could Justin, if he were here today, say of this generation, "And many, both men and women, who have been Christ's disciples from childhood, have preserved their purity at the age of sixty or seventy years; and I am proud that I could produce such from every race of men and women" (ch. 15)?

CHAPTERS 21–22: PAGAN FABLES VERSUS RATIONAL BELIEF IN CHRIST

In chapters 21–29, Justin proved the irrationality of paganism when compared with Christianity. The first section deals with pagan fables. Justin's first agenda was to address the question of Jesus Christ's conception and subsequent birth without sexual union, a matter questioned by his readers. In his answer, Justin said that Christian belief is more rational than the fables to which all of them currently ascribe.

He cited several examples: Hermes, Asclepius, Dionysus, Heracles, Dioscori, Perseus, and Bellerophon, the latter of which, though born of mortal union, rose into heaven on a horse. Others among the group ascended into heaven or committed themselves to flames to escape the pains of mortality. Ariadne was placed among the stars. It was even alleged that emperors rose into heaven from their funeral pyres.

In citing these examples from their own beliefs, Justin made clear that Christianity is not irrational from their own standpoint. What is dramatically different about Christ, however, is His sinless life when compared with the likes of Zeus, for example. The tales of Zeus include wanton degradation of others, the love of evil, and generations of children who killed their parents. How can Zeus represent holiness and virtue? Justin reminded his hearers that those who live unjustly and do not change their ways "are punished in eternal fire" (ch. 21).

Justin's next step was to show the superiority of Christ over other gods. Jesus was better than Hermes, said to be the announcing word from God; He was better than the sons of Zeus who suffered different kinds of cruel deaths, even though His was by Crucifixion; He was better than Perseus, said to have been born of a virgin; and He was better than Asclepius, who was said to have healed the lame, the paralytic, and the blind. How was He better? His deeds clearly set Him apart (ch. 22).

Tried but . . .

"It is not that Christianity has been tried and found wanting, but that Christianity has been found difficult, and not tried at all."—G. K. Chesterton

CHAPTER 23: DIVINITY OF CHRIST

Justin focused on the three reasons Christ is above the rest. First, the story of Jesus Christ was prophesied long before the other fables were written, and His story has been proven to be true. Second, the Savior alone was "real begotten as Son by God, being His Word and First-begotten and Power." He became man because of His own will for the conversion of the human race. Third, before Christ came to earth, there was demonic activity that blinded the hearts of people so that myths were established, which even Justin's readers now believed to be true (ch. 23). These demons also spread scandalous reports against Christians, which Justin refuted in the following section.

CHAPTERS 24–29: INTOLERANCE OF IMPOSTERS IMPLORED

Here Justin names the unproven accusations against Christians. First, followers of Christ are hated for their name alone and are put to death as sinners even though they have done no wrong. Others, Justin noted, worship trees, rivers, mice, cats, crocodiles, and other "irrational animals" and are not put to death, even though none of these is equally honored. Yet Christians are put to death for not worshiping the same gods as other empire citizens. Justin said this is ludicrous! All empire citizens do not worship the same gods (ch 24)!

Second, Justin called attention to the Christians who were converted out of Greek or Roman pantheon worship, who used to sacrifice to deities with uncontrolled sexual passions, or greed, or murderous hatred. He bid his readers look at Christ, who never "was goaded by lust for Antiope, or such other women, or of Ganymede, nor was He delivered of that hundred-handed mon-

Unwanted Children

Early Christian and pagan literature abound with references to the practice of discarding unwanted children. Sometimes infants were aborted; sometimes children were exposed to die after they were born and their sex was determined. Some of these died. Others were snatched up by those who raised them for purposes of prostitution and other "unspeakable iniquities." A note written by a husband to his wife in year A.D. 1 said, "If you are delivered of a male child, let it live; if of a female, expose it" (*Oxyrhynchus Papyri, 4.744*).

ster" over the matter of a concubine. Justin said he pitied those who worship these ineffective gods (ch. 25).

In the following section, Justin argued that many false teachers have gained followers, some of whom have even been recognized by the Roman authorities. One such teacher was Simon, who went about with his formerly public prostitute, Helena, together with their disciple, Menander. Simon of Samaria was mentioned briefly in Acts 8:9–25, where he professed to believe in Christ when Philip was preaching. Afterwards, he tried to purchase the power of the Holy Spirit from Peter and John.

Marcion is another that Justin mentioned in this paragraph, who teaches that there is a greater god than the "Maker of this Universe." Justin's point in this litany was to say that not all persons who claim to be of Christ actually belong to Him, one of Justin's recurring themes. These false teachers give nonbelievers misinformation about what true Christians believe. And yet, even these are not put to death for their beliefs (ch. 27).

There are, however, beliefs associated with pagans that Christians abhor. These Justin enumerated. He first pointed to the common custom of "exposing children," which he associated with murder. If the children lived, it often resulted in both girls and boys growing up into prostitution. Justin used strong words to demonstrate his disgust for these and other pagan practices, some with regard to their own children and wives, including the mutilation of one's children for the purposes of homosexuality (ch. 27).

Simon Rebuked by Peter

When Simon, the magician from Samaria, tried to purchase the power of the Holy Spirit from Peter and John, Peter answered him sternly, "May your money perish with you, because you thought you could buy the gift of God with money! You have no part or share in this ministry, because your heart is not right before God. Repent of this wickedness and pray to the Lord. Perhaps He will forgive you for having such a thought in your heart. For I see that you are full of bitterness and captive to sin" (Acts 8:18–23, NIV). This man spawned a new term for the sale of ecclesiastical posts, or the profit made in selling sacred things, or trying to buy the conferring of the Holy Spirit—*simony*.

Justin next spoke of the association pagan worship had with snakes and the revolt that Christians felt toward worship of this creature. Since the snake represents to Christians the person of Satan, they knew him to be "the leader of the evil demons" and the source of all wickedness (ch. 28).

The last topic of this section deals with Christian marriage. One of its purposes, said Justin, is for the procreation and nurturing of children. Promiscuity is not a Christian practice. In fact, many Christians choose not to marry and live perfectly content as virgins. He cited as an example one young man that recently petitioned Felix, Prefect in Alexandria, for permission so that local physicians could make him a voluntary eunuch. He did this sincerely in order to follow what he perceived to be Christ's command in Matthew 19:12, an issue with which Origen also dealt. In this case, says Justin, Felix denied the request, whereupon the youth was content "with the testimony of his own conscience" (ch. 29).

Origen's Decision to be Chaste

Origen (c. 185–254) of Alexandria was born to Christian parents. His father, Leonidas, was martyred in 202, after which Origen taught in the catechetical school there. When he was a young man, Origen emasculated himself, misinterpreting Matthew 19:12 in a literal sense. He founded a famous school in Caesarea, where he taught and preached. One of the most prolific writers of the church fathers and author of the first systematic theology, called *On First Principles*, he was persecuted under Decius in 250 and died as the result of his prolonged torture not long thereafter.

 COMMENTARY

Superiority of Christianity over Paganism. Justin clearly used these chapters to extol the virtues of Christianity by painting two pictures—one of comparison and the other of contrast. He left little of paganism's ugliness covered here. With broad strokes of his pen, Justin painted the truth about inconsistency, wickedness, and deception which were evident in pagan thought and practice.

Justin's knowledge of mythology was essential for his role as defender of the Christian faith.

With keen ability and shrewd insight, Justin pointed to those areas of comparison with pagan religions. He showed where other pagan deities are reported to be virgin-born, descended from gods, tortured to death in different ways, ascended to heaven, or descended into the pit of flames. Almost all of the facts of the gospel story have been counterfeited, said Justin, and are reproduced in the multiple myths created by Satan and his demons to confuse human beings. After making this point clear, Justin drove home his point that these beliefs in and of themselves do not merit punishment unto death. Indeed, pagans are encouraged and honored for holding such beliefs. What makes Christians any different?

The second tactic Justin took was to show the superiority of Christianity by way of contrast. Pagans lived such degraded lives, he stated. The treatment of children and the powerless were held as examples of such depravity, while Christian virtues were held up in stark relief. Justin's last thrust concerning the recently departed Antinous, whose dubious relationship with Hadrian had been the cause of much speculation, is most significant.

At the untimely drowning of his close favorite in 130, Hadrian had built a new city on the site of his death and initiated a cult for his worship. The cult of Antinous had grown rapidly in the two decades since, giving rise to Justin's jab, "And it is not out of place, we think, to mention here Antinous, who was recently alive, and whom everybody . . . hastened to worship as a god, though they knew both who he was and what was his origin" (ch. 29). Following as it does the story of the chaste youth who was content to remain a virgin, Justin's remarks here

A thoughtful response to Justin's arguments calls for soul-searching on the part of contemporary Christians. In America, Christians are protected by law from physical persecution because of choosing a particular creed or faith. Rarely do followers of Christ give up their lives for the gospel on home turf. Yet what if all true Christians began a wholesale, combined effort to confront behavior that was morally and biblically wrong? Would there be any backlash against Christians? What about the modern equivalents of "exposure" and prostitution? These practices were considered unconscionable for Christians of the second century. Justin's words cut through the intervening centuries to speak to this generation as it deals with many of the same evils.

were no accident. This is an audacious public challenge from Justin to Antoninus Pius, son of Hadrian, who knew of his father's attachment to the youth.

CHAPTERS 30–53: PROOFS OF PROPHECY FULFILLED

Justin set the stage for the next section by asking the logical questions that might be in the minds of his readers: What keeps the man we call Christ from being a mere dabbler in magical arts? How do His followers know that He was indeed who He claimed to be? These answers, Justin asserted, may be found in ancient prophecy, the "strongest and surest evidence" (ch. 30).

Justin shared his love of history in this passage. The prophetic Spirit of God came upon many Jewish prophets, who foretold events of the gospel story, Justin explained. These Jews preserved the prophecies in their collected writings, handing down the books to successive generations. When Ptolemy collected these writings and sent for translators, the prophecies came into the Greek language and were found there. These predictions came to pass: the virgin birth; growing to manhood; healing diseases; raising the dead; being hated, unrecognized, and crucified; dying and rising again; ascending into heaven; and "both being and being called Son of God." Justin told his readers that prophecies regularly came—at five thousand, three thousand, two thousand, one thousand, and eight hundred years before Christ (ch. 31).

Chapter 32 centers on Moses' statements in Genesis 49:10–11 about the Messiah coming from the house of Judah, and washing his garments in the blood of the grape. Chapter 33

Famous Library at Alexandria

Alexandria was the second city of the Roman Empire, a center of both Hellenistic and Jewish culture. It was home to the largest community of Jews in the world. Ptolemy Philadelphus (285–246 B.C.) desired a copy of the Hebrew Law for his great library at Alexandria. He sent word to Herod of Judea; it was promptly delivered. Next, Ptolemy needed translators, and so 72 were sent, hence the name, LXX. Over the next hundred years, the Septuagint was translated. This was the version of the Old Testament used by the early church. New Testament writers quoted from it. As an interesting side note, Paul never preached in Alexandria.

focuses on the virgin birth from Isaiah 7:14, repeated in Matthew 1:23. Chapter 34 deals with Micah's prophecy concerning Bethlehem as the birthplace of Christ in Micah 5:2, echoed in Matthew 2:6. As to the prophecies of Jesus' growth to manhood, Justin quoted and explained the passage in Isaiah 9:6, "For unto us a child is born" (ch. 35).

In chapters 36–42, Justin demonstrated how the prophetic voice speaks. The writers themselves had no words of their own, but the "divine Word" moved through them. Sometimes God the Father spoke; sometimes it was Christ, and still other times it was "the people answering the Lord or His Father." Justin then gave by example the places where each of these occurs in Scripture, citing no references but summarizing the texts.

Chapter 43 denies what some questioned to be simple, inevitable destiny. He argued for free choice in decision making. Unless the human race has power by free choice to avoid evil and to choose good, there is no responsibility for actions, whatever kind they may be. Indeed, he is clear on this point: "But this we assert is irrevocable destiny, that those who choose the good have deserved rewards, and those who choose the opposite have their just punishment."

The subject of good and evil follows in the next chapter, as Justin reviewed the prophets' statements about the choice between choosing blessing and cursing. First with Moses, and next with Isaiah, Justin pointed to the truths which, in later years, philosophers picked up and explained in their reasoning (ch. 44).

The final emphasis of this argument is that Christ would sit at the right hand of the Father.

"The scepter shall not depart from Judah, Nor the ruler's staff from between his feet, Until Shiloh comes, And to him shall be the obedience of the peoples.

He ties his foal to the vine,

And his donkey's colt to the choice vine;

He washes his garments in wine, And his robes in the blood of grapes."

(Gen. 49:10–11, NASB).

Here Justin pictured Christ as the resurrected Victor, whose power and authority are unquestioned from prophecy. In this moment, Justin allowed himself the opportunity to reiterate the fate of those who, knowing the truth, refuse to accept it. He said, "And if you also will read these words in a hostile spirit, you can do no more, as we said before, than kill us; which indeed does no harm to us, but to you and all who unjustly are enemies, and do not repent, brings eternal punishment by fire" (ch. 45).

Human Beings Are Not Trees

"For God did not make a man or a woman like other things, such as trees and animals, which cannot act by choice; for neither would he be worthy of rewards or praise if he did not choose the good of himself, having been born so; nor, if he were evil, would he be worthy of punishment, not being evil himself, but being unable to be anything other than that for which he was born" (Ch. 43).

A new question arises in chapter 46. In fact, Justin anticipated the logical thesis that there must have been no salvation for those who lived before the time of Christ. Here Justin made the cogent argument that there were indeed Christians before Christ and states his case through the lenses of his *logos* concept. According to Justin, anyone who "lived with the *logos* are Christians," even if they were formerly considered atheists. He pointed to Greeks, such as Socrates and Heraclitus, and to Abraham, Ananias, Asarias, Mishael, the latter three Hebrews, who were given Babylonian names and thrown into the fiery furnace. This cluster refers to persons Justin believed to have renounced idolatry. They must, then, be accounted with those who were persecuted for the sake of righteousness.

Chapters 47–51 continue the theme of prophecies fulfilled. The land of Judah would be lain waste; Christ would heal diseases; the Jews would not recognize Christ as their long-awaited Messiah; He would endure sufferings and dishonor; He would rise from the dead; He would bear away the sins of the world; and, someday, He would return triumphant.

Justin saved chapter 52 for the ringing confidence that since many prophecies foretold have already come to pass it follows that those which remain will also surely be fulfilled. The prophets told of two comings. The first has already happened. This leaves the second, which will take place just as fully as has been predicted. When this occurs, the living and the dead will be judged. The worthy will be clothed with incorruption (see 1 Cor. 15:53), and the wicked, eternally conscious, will spend eternity with the wicked demons.

The last segment summarizes all that Justin said about prophecy. His closing words speak to the huge numbers of Gentiles who have fulfilled the prophecies concerning those who would become followers of the Christ. Citing Isaiah, but correctly meaning Jeremiah 9:26, Justin quoted, "Israel is uncircumcised in heart, but the Gentiles are uncircumcised [in the flesh]." He believed that all of these many things are sufficient to implant conviction and faith in those who welcome the truth, who are not governed by their passions and egos (ch. 53).

COMMENTARY

Arguments for Prophecy. This treatise on fulfilled prophecy is the longest running argument of *First Apology*. Justin began with Moses and covered the elements of the gospel topically, almost chronologically. The fulfilled prophecies surrounding Christ's lineage, purpose, birth, nationality, obscurity, authority, manner of death, glorious Resurrection, and soon coming mount an impressive body of evidence against those who would deprecate the faith Justin represented.

The insertion of Trinitarian voices into the litany shows his clear distinction between the persons of the Trinity, although no relationship is explained. His purpose, however, is to demonstrate how the Old Testament sings forth an audible refrain of the coming Messiah. This he does admirably, although he is quick to say that the Jews did not have ears to hear its song. Instead, the Gentiles heard and responded as, indeed, had been foretold.

This is significant, for Justin hit a chord that has resounded throughout the history of the church since the Resurrection. That the gospel is for all persons everywhere, regardless of nationality, financial status, color, or gender, is perhaps the greatest wonder of all. The message of Christ crosses over all boundaries; it is the only one of its kind. Gentiles have responded. Today, almost two thousand years later, two billion of the earth's five billion inhabitants claim to be Christian.[7] The Roman authorities would perhaps have been in awe to consider the staggering numbers that would one day profess the same faith they were trying, in Justin's age, to silence.

CHAPTERS 54–58: MYTHOLOGY AND CHRIST

Justin took the offense in this section, showing that the myths of pagan religions not only have no proof to offer youths but also are untenable in and of themselves. These myths, Justin believed, have been created for the human race by demons so that men might be deceived and kept from recognizing and following Christ.

Justin began again with Moses, "older than all writers," to begin his task. When Moses wrote that Jesus would wash His garments in the blood of the vine, the demons created a myth of Dionysius, the god of wine, who would ascend into heaven. When Moses wrote that He would come mounted on a foal, a myth stated that it was Bellerophon who rode his horse, Pegasus, into the clouds. When Isaiah foretold that Christ would be born of a virgin, Perseus became the pure one of legendary fame. When Psalm 19:5 described Christ as a "giant to run his course," the myth of Heracles arose; and when it was prophesied that He would heal all diseases, the demons ascribed this work to Asclepius (ch. 54).

In the next passage, Justin drew a fascinating parallel. It centers on the single universal symbol of Christianity—the cross. Justin found the cross figure in every aspect of the cosmos, as if God undergirded the universe with this visual reminder of history's pivotal event. Justin found the cross in a mast and sail, as a boat skims its way across the water; in the tools of the farmer or artisan, who digs the earth and carves the wood; in the human form itself, arms outstretched and head erect; in the planes of the face, where the nose draws the breath of life and the line of the eyes and brows bisects its length. Yet nowhere did the myths replicate the story of the cross, pointed out Justin. This, then, "is the greatest symbol of His power and rule, as also is shown from the things which fall under view" (ch. 55).

The wicked demons continued their despoiling, creating counterfeit miracle-workers like Simon the magician, who so deceived the people that even the Roman Sacred Senate was taken in and erected a statue to his honor. Justin called for the statue to be destroyed. He noted that Menander and Marcion are two more deceivers

Anti-Christian Graffiti

The earliest known anti-Christian graffiti (c. 200) comes from the Palatine, the largest of Rome's seven hills. The symbol etched there represented a cross with the crucified having a donkey's head. The inscription reads, "Alexamenos worships his god."

like Simon, who cause others to fall prey to godless teachings and that evil plots to kill the followers of Christ eventuate from the same depraved work (ch. 56–58). People listen to their irrational teaching and, like lambs snatched away by wolves, are led astray.

CHAPTERS 59–60: PLATO, MOSES, AND THE CREATION STORY

In chapter 59, Justin plainly stated that Plato "took his statement that God made the Universe by changing formless matter" from Moses: "In the beginning God made the heaven and the earth. And the earth was invisible and unfurnished, and darkness was over the abyss; and the Spirit of God moved over the waters. And God said, let there be light. And it was so." In this way Justin said that he himself, Plato, and anyone else can learn that the whole universe came into being by the Word of God out of the substratum spoken of by Moses.

Plato's *Timaeus* gathered its physiological discussion of the Son of God from Moses as well, Justin claimed. From the story of Moses' lifting up the rod in the wilderness, causing the poisonous snakes to die, Plato identified the *Chi* power which, he said, "was placed *Chi-wise* in the universe." Plato, therefore, had a seed of the *logos* as he wrote and thought. Plato's writings can point people to Christ, for even the ignorant echo the truth found in the prophecies about Him.

 COMMENTARY

Paganism's Imitation of Christianity. In the section above, the last discussion of paganism in Justin Martyr's *First Apology*, the writer wrote convincingly of the deficiencies of the mythological stories. By tracing the partial shadows of the Christ-story in the pagan legends, Justin demonstrated how people have been blinded by evil design. Herein lies a simple but profound message. Half-truths always lead away from truth, not toward it; yet somehow human beings seem to prefer the lie.

What are some contemporary half-truths that have the potential of leading people away from Christ?

This is a cold assessment of the human condition in a fallen world. For all that the latest technology and scientific discovery have brought to the globe, it is no less fallen today than it was when Justin wrote so poignantly of humankind's refusal to recognize Christ as Savior in his day. Nevertheless, he pointed his readers away from half-lies to the whole truth compacted in the cross of Christ.

Justin's word pictures about the Cross have staggering impact. When one begins to look for the Cross, it may be found everywhere. Even though his Middle Platonistic worldview is hard to miss here, Justin reduced the essence of the Christian experience into just one word—the Cross. Upon the Cross, then, the entire centrality of the gospel message hinges. It is the irreducible core of Christianity. No wonder Justin remarked that its message has never been duplicated. Impossible for a nonbeliever to understand, this symbol of gruesome, agonizing, and violent death is the focal point of history. This is what makes the interactive narrative between God and humans truly His-story.

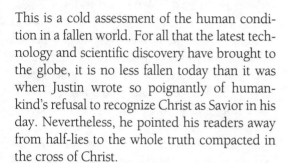

Paul, writing to the Galatians said, "As for me, God forbid that I should boast about anything except the cross of our Lord Jesus Christ. Because of that cross, my interest in this world died long ago, and the world's interest in me is also long dead" (Gal. 6:14, NLT).

CHAPTERS 61–67: CHRISTIAN BAPTISM AND COMMUNION

Justin's final series of topics deal with the subject of Christian observances, ordinances, or sacraments. So that there would be no mistake,

Baptismal Questions

Hippolytus (c. 215) reported the following queries, while the candidate was in the water:
Question: "Dost thou believe in God, the Father Almighty?"
Answer: "I believe;" and the candidate was baptized once.

Next question: "Dost thou believe in Christ Jesus, the Son of God, who was born by the Holy Ghost of the Virgin Mary, was crucified under Pontius Pilate, was dead and buried, and rose again the third day, alive from the dead, and ascended into heaven, and sat down at the right hand of the Father, and will come to judge the quick and the dead?"
Answer: "I believe;" then the candidate was immersed a second time.

Third question: "Dost thou believe in the Holy Ghost, in the holy church, and the resurrection of the flesh?"
Final answer: "I believe;" whereupon the candidate was baptized the third time.

Justin explained what Christians do when they gather together. There were no "mystery rites" here, no foundation for speculation.

Chapter 61 explains how the body of believers accepted new converts. When someone believed "that the things we say and teach are true," and wished to live accordingly, they prayed and fasted, asking God to forgive past sins. Fellow believers also prayed and fasted with her. Then the new convert, after a period of catechism, was brought away to the place of baptism, where she was baptized, signifying her new birth. This took place in the name of "God the Father and Master of all, and of our Savior, Jesus Christ, and of the Holy Spirit." At this time, Justin believed, the new convert is illuminated with the transforming power of God unto good works which, if nurtured and obeyed, will result in righteous living.

Justin then wrote a parenthesis, as if a new thought crossed his mind, about the pagan rites which followed from this Christian rite of baptism. Temple worship consisted of pouring libations, ritual cleansing, sprinkling, and removing shoes; the latter practice, Justin said, came from the story of Moses and the burning bush (ch. 62–63). He reiterates his view that the pagan goddess Kore, daughter of Zeus, was taken from the creation story of the Spirit of God moving over the waters, and that Athena, another daughter of Zeus, was called the "first thought" after the concept of *logos* in Scripture (ch. 64).

After the new convert has been baptized, Justin continued with his previous line of thought, she is brought before the gathered believers, who welcome her and pray for the whole assembly and for "all others everywhere." They exchange a kiss of peace, after which the new believer receives Communion for the first time. The "Ruler" receives the bread and the cup of mixed water and wine, says a lengthy prayer of gratitude, and all of the people say "Amen." The deacons then distribute the bread and cup to all who are present, then take it to those who are absent (ch. 66).

Justin defined the nature of the "food [which] is called among us Eucharist" (ch. 66). No persons are allowed to partake of the bread and wine except those who believe in Christ and His teachings, who have received Christian baptism, and who have shown themselves to be obedient to Him. Justin referred to the initiation rites of Mithraism, which also included the taking of bread and water, with secret words said over them.

After the Communion rite, the more wealthy of their number share their material possessions with the poor. On Sundays, believers gather to hear the Scripture read aloud, which Justin called "the memoirs of the Apostles " and "the writings of the prophets," (ch. 67). Then the Ruler delivers "a discourse [which] instructs and exhorts [the listeners] to the imitation of these good things." Then all stand up together and offer prayer, followed by the rite of Communion as described above.

The deacons also carry the elements to the absent members on Sundays. An offering is taken up for the poor, which is distributed to the orphans, widows, those who are sick, in need, "in bonds," or who are strangers in their midst. Justin said this "first day" service on Sunday takes place to celebrate the Creation of the world and the Resurrection of Christ.

An Early Easter Hymn

In Justin's day, the church likely interspersed the chanting of psalms among the different Scripture readings. Congregational prayer sometimes took the form of chanting as well. This one, celebrating Easter, was written by Melito, Bishop of Sardis (d. 190): "The mystery of the Pasch is new and old, eternal and temporal, corruptible and incorruptible, mortal and immortal . . . Born as Son, led like a lamb, sacrificed like a sheep, buried as a man, he rises from the dead as God, being by nature both God and man. He is all things: when he judges, he is law; when he teaches, word; when he saves, grace; when he begets, father; when he is begotten, son; when he suffers, lamb; when he is buried, man; when he arises, God. Such is Christ! To him be glory forever! Amen."

CHAPTER 68: CONCLUSION

In his closing remarks, Justin bid his readers to respect *First Apology* if it seems reasonable and true. If it seems nothing but nonsense, he begged the authorities to treat it as such and not to decree death to those who believe it. His tone then changed somewhat, reminding them that they would not escape the judgment of Almighty God if they persist in their injustice. While Christians could demand a formal hearing, based on a decree handed down by Emperor Hadrian, which Justin appended to this treatise, Christians wish first to explain their position in hopes that tolerance, even protection, be afforded them (ch. 68).

 COMMENTARY

Church Ordinances and Order. If Justin could have invited the Roman emperor, his top staff, state administrators, senators, and all other notables to church, they could have observed what he described in detail in his final paragraphs. Here his readers get a glimpse of the early church as it conducted its services, received new converts, baptized, and received the Lord's Supper. Justin did not record for his readers what hymns were sung or what specific Scripture passages were read. He defined neither "ruler" nor "deacon." Yet this is one of the earliest accounts of church life outside the New Testament.

This view of second-century church order is important, for it is one of the few extant sources which reveal how the early church "did church." Because of this account, contemporary Christians have the opportunity to compare their own practices with those of Justin's

Give Us This Day Our Daily Bread

Soon after Justin Martyr's era, Christians in North Africa took one step further the practice of delivering Communion to the homes of those who were absent. Church members began taking home the bread so they could celebrate the Lord's Supper every day. Squabbles soon erupted as people began to misuse this practice.

day. Is baptism still for those who are believers only? Does the rite of baptism follow a period of thorough instruction? Does the church family pray and fast with the catechumen prior to the baptismal service? Does the service end with thanksgiving and praise, followed by the Lord's Supper?

QUESTIONS TO GUIDE YOUR STUDY

1. What do you think compelled Justin to be the spokesman for Christianity in his day?

2. What qualified him for the task?

3. Is there a need for such a stand today? Who could be that voice?

4. In our day there are hundreds of belief systems parading as the truth. What can Justin Martyr teach us about the importance of knowing what others believe?

5. Why should accurate communication of the gospel message be a priority for believers?

6. In explaining Christianity to nonbelievers, Justin Martyr felt free to borrow cultural language and ideas from his world. Is this a valid premise for effective dialogue? If so, what might be some cultural commonalties that might effectively communicate theological truth to nonbelievers? What might be the dangers in adaptation?

7. What elements of Christian worship were most significant for Justin Martyr? If you were asked to summarize, in three paragraphs, an account of your worship, baptismal, and Communion services, what details would you include? Why?

Justin also gave clear expectations for those receiving the Communion rite. His three are these prerequisites—faith, baptism, and obedience to Christ. Are these still valid today? Does the church family today hear the Scriptures read aloud followed by a sermon that spurs the fellowship to "imitate good things"? Do the people of God still offer up prayer and thanksgiving "to the best of their ability"? Is an offering distributed to those who are widows, orphans, needy, sick, strangers, and in prison? Does the body of Christ still meet on the first day to signify Creation and the Resurrection? After reading Justin, these and other questions prompt Christians to examine afresh their own expressions of faith.

"And we therefore ask you to publish this petition, appending what you think right, that our opinions may be known to others" (ch. 14).

DATE, AUDIENCE, AND PURPOSE

Dating the *Second Apology* is more problematic than the *First Apology*. It cannot have been written much after 151–55, since Justin Martyr said in *Second* that the *First* was newly written. He also referred to Anoninus Pius as emperor and spoke of Marcus Aurelius as a pious philosopher.

Eusebius on Justin

"This Justin has left us many monuments of a mind well stored with learning, and devoted to sacred things, replete with matter profitable in every respect. To these we shall refer our readers, only indicating as we proceed, those that have come to our knowledge.... These we deemed necessary to state, in order to stimulate the studious likewise to the diligent perusal of these books. And thus much respecting Justin."—Eusebius of Caesarea, Historian, *Ecclesiastical History*, 18.

The problem arises when Eusebius mentioned that Justin had written two Apologies, one during the reign of Antoninus Pius and the other under his son, Antoninus Verus, or Marcus Aurelius. Yet *Second Apology* notes that Antoninus Pius was sole emperor at the time, just as he had been when *First* was written. It seems probable that either Eusebius made a mistake in citing Pius, rather than Verus, as emperor or that another work was written later, which is now no longer extant.

This would be logical, especially since Eusebius quoted from what are now called *First* and *Second Apology* but described these as both coming from *First Apology*. It seems then, that what is now called *First* and *Second Apology* Eusebius knew as *First Apology* and that the second volume of which he spoke has been lost. Was the *Second Apology* a preface to the *First*? Was it perhaps an appendage to the end? This seems most likely. It was common in Justin Martyr's day for writers to attach several smaller works together and publish them as one volume.

As to audience, *Second Apology* has no other salutation than that which appears at its head: "Addressed to the Roman Senate." The *Second Apology* is a different genre of literature than the *First*. Its prose expresses Justin's outrage with the injustices about which he has been hearing. Apparently, a recent indignity had been inflicted upon a Christian teacher named Ptolemaeus. This is a passionate appeal for action, an angry response to a specific event.

Although *Second Apology* is much shorter than *First*, only fifteen chapters as compared to sixty-eight, Justin Martyr's purpose is clear. In the face of mounting pressure, Justin was convinced that believers should stand firm against hatred without retreat. This, for him, was the essential Christian quality.

SECOND APOLOGY AT A GLANCE

Chapters 1–2	Situation in Rome Explained
Chapter 3	Malice of Those Who Hate Christians
Chapters 4–9	Answers to Questions About Christianity
Chapters 10–12	Christians and Suffering
Chapter 13	Christianity as Completed Philosophy
Chapters 14–15	Authorization of Writings

CHAPTERS 1–2: SITUATION IN ROME EXPLAINED

In his opening statements, Justin addressed the Romans inclusively. Under the prefect Urbicus, some dreadful injustice had been committed, compelling Justin to enter a strong protest with the authorities. He hastened to explain himself (ch. 1). Apparently, a formerly intemperate woman had become a believer and had learned to live soberly. She began persuading her non-believing husband about his need to live rightly and assuring him of impending eternal punishment should he not conform his life to the teachings of Christ and right reason.

This angered the husband, who continued to alienate his wife by his extravagances. She, in turn, feeling it morally wrong to live any longer as a wife with such a husband, wished to be divorced from him. Her Christian friends begged her to stay with him that he might one day experience conversion. Meanwhile, the husband went to Alexandria and conducted himself worse than ever before. The wife, feeling that to continue to share his table and bed would cause her to be guilty of the same profligacy by association, presented him with a bill of divorcement and was separated from him.

The husband responded by charging her publicly with the crime of being a Christian. The wife petitioned Emperor Antoninus Pius for time to settle her affairs and then prepare a defense against the charge. Both requests were granted. In the meantime, the husband turned his wrath on the Christian teacher Ptolemaeus, his wife's discipler in the faith. Ptolemaeus was thrown into prison and kept there for some time, where he was repeatedly questioned about whether he was a Christian. Ptolemaeus always answered that he was.

When Urbicus had Ptolemaeus put in prison, Lucius, who was a Christian himself, accused Urbicus of injustice: "Why have you punished this man, not as an adulterer, nor fornicator, nor

Divorce in Rome

Contrary to Jewish law, which allowed men to divorce their wives but not vice versa, Roman law allowed women to divorce their husbands. The church had its own law concerning divorce, which was not recognized if the marriage was consummated.

murderer, nor thief, nor robber, nor convicted of any crime at all, but as one who has only confessed that he is called by the name of Christian?" Lucius concluded by charging that the judgment did not reflect well on Emperor Pius, the Sacred Senate, or Marcus Aurelius. At this point, Urbicus suspected Lucius' leanings and asked him if he was a Christian also. "Most certainly I am," he replied. Then Lucius was led away to punishment along with a third who had come forward (ch. 2).

CHAPTER 3: MALICE OF THOSE WHO HATE CHRISTIANS

In the next section, without further explanation to the above story, Justin revealed that he felt certain of impending arrest and punishment on the rack. This might be at the hands of some of these already named, he said, or a man named Crescens, who was a foolish aspirant to philosophy. Justin admitted to having trounced the Cynic Crescens in public debate and offered to do so again before the authorities, should Crescens bring to them any accusation (ch. 3).

 COMMENTARY

Hatred Against Christians. Justin's first words recall the salutation of Socrates: "O Romans," he hailed, heralding the emperor, senate, soldiers, and citizenry in the single term. In the first two sections, Justin Martyr showed remarkable calm in relating both an event that had already taken place and one he felt was forthcoming.

The story Justin related is an interesting one, opening the windows to a second-century marriage and showing the intricacies involved in

Ignorance Exposed

"I . . . am expecting to be plotted against and fixed to a rack . . . perhaps by Crescens, that lover of bravado and boasting. For the man is unworthy of the name *philosopher* who publicly bears witness against us in matters which he does not understand, saying that Christians are godless and impious, and doing so to win favor with the deluded mob. . . . For if he runs us down without having read the teachings of Christ, he is thoroughly evil, and far worse than the inexperienced people, who often refrain from discussing or bearing false witness about matters they do not understand" (ch. 2).

relationship problem solving. Almost behind the scenes, readers learn how one family was unable to come to a biblical resolution in the short term. Justin also revealed two aspects of state intervention—one with just results, the emperor's judgment in favor of the wife; and the other without justice, the decisions against believers. Without remarking on the situation, Justin recounted the tale dispassionately, concerned primarily that his readers learn the fates of Ptolemaeus and Lucius. This had already happened. The other event was still to come.

What is the response of today's believers toward ignorance resulting in hatred of Christians? What is your personal response?

Justin Martyr knew his days were short, although he did not share how he became aware of this. Like other church leaders to follow, such as Polycarp, Perpetua, and Saturus, Justin had been forewarned of his approaching death. He knew it would be bearable, however, and set his face to finish his course until that time arrived.

Together, these two sections demonstrate the increasing antagonism of the Roman State against Christians and the injustice accorded them once they were accused. Through simple testimony of a neighbor, family member, or enemy, Christians could be brought to punishment, even death, without a fair trial.

CHAPTERS 4–9: ANSWERS TO QUESTIONS ABOUT CHRISTIANS

Justin anticipated the question of a weary consul in his next paragraph: "But lest anyone should say, 'Go then all of you and commit suicide, and pass even now to God, and do not trouble us,'—I will tell you why we do not do so." Justin reminded his readers that God made the world for the human race. He wishes His people to live good and pure lives unto Him. If the Christians should perish, said Justin, then they would in fact be removing the cause for God's blessing to remain on the Earth. In effect, Christians live so that others may be blessed and so that this gospel message might spread (ch. 4).

To the suggestion that Christians should pray to God for help, so that punishments should cease, Justin reiterated his belief that demons cause the wickedness perpetrated against them. This takes place according the natural order that God instituted at Creation (ch. 5). In opposition to this evil design stands the eternal *logos*, who came to set men free from their deeds.

Chapter 6 deals again with Justin's theme of *logos*, the Son of God, the Christ and Sower of the *logos*, who was present at Creation and reveals God to humankind. Through His power Christians regularly exorcise demons from captive humanity, said Justin, and bid his readers to recognize this power and watch to see how believers heal the sick in Christ's name.

If Christians did not live upon the Earth, Justin argued, the fire of judgment would descend and dissolve all things. The seedlings of the *logos* may be found in the believers, and through them preservation and life extend to others on the planet. Stoics do not have the right idea; no fate governs the world. Instead, "this is the nature of all that is made—to be capable of vice and virtue." People must choose to live rightly; else they will experience destruction, just as did the generation killed by the great Flood (ch. 7).

For Justin, the seeds of the *logos* may also be discerned in all former philosophers who were persecuted for seeking after virtue and shunning vice. Justin mentioned two in this discourse: Heraclitus and Musonius, the latter of whom was killed in Justin's lifetime. Some may think,

On Christian Influences

"They are crocuses in the winter of a fallen world."—Hendrikus Berkhof.

said Justin, that the prospect of eternal destruction for the wicked is nothing more than a scare tactic. This is most assuredly not so. The evil ones make men vacillate as to what is considered right and wrong, confusing laws and standards for righteousness. Judgment is coming nonetheless, he reminded his hearers, and humankind's required accountability before God does not change with the notions of men (ch. 8–9).

CHAPTERS 10–12: CHRISTIANS AND SUFFERING

In chapter 10, Justin called Christ the "whole rational principle . . ., who appeared for our sake, body, and reason, and soul." Before He assumed the human nature, anything "uttered well" by former lawgivers or philosophers contained seeds of the *logos*, even though such persons could not contemplate or investigate fully who Christ was. But when Christ came in the flesh, scholars, artisans, peasants, educated and base, believed in Him because He was God's *logos* fully revealed.

Justin moved on in the next section to consider death, the "debt due from every person who has been born." He related the story of Heracles found in Xenophon and his three choices. Vice compelled him to follow her seductive pleasure where all would be splendor and beauty. Virtue, a woman "of squalid look and dress," promised that to choose her would ensure not passing beauty but "everlasting and precious graces." Justin made the point that vice often deceives, enslaving people to a lie. They think vice will bring to them only that which truly belongs to virtue. Virtue brings everlasting beauty and incorruptibility, and therefore death holds no power over the believer. People suffer because discipline and probation bring blessedness (ch. 11).

In chapter 12, the last of this theme, Justin related the amazing peace Christians show in the face of death. Indeed, they would rather leave this life than give a false report to save it; they would state their allegiance to Christ rather than purchase their freedom with a lie. Horrible evils became associated with Christianity because of the work of evil ones, who tortured children or weaker female slaves, forcing from them false confessions. Yet even when Christians were unjustly put to death for these ludicrous crimes, Justin said, they showed no fear. They were athletes, who prove their virtue by flaunting death.

Shouting Down the Enemy

"But would that . . . someone would mount a lofty rostrum, and shout with a tragic voice, 'Be ashamed, be ashamed, you who charge the guiltless with those deeds which you yourselves openly commit, and who ascribe things which refer to yourselves, and to your gods to those who have no part in them. Be converted, become wise'" (ch. 13).

 COMMENTARY

Questions, Suffering, and Death. Justin found noble themes in this section; his questions deal with Christians' views about life and death. He portrayed Christians as having no fear, the perfect foil for all who would falsely accuse them of wrongdoing. This is his crystallizing point. For Justin, facing hatred, accusers, or even death, without flinching, was the mark of true Christianity.

This theme of Christian persecution runs deep throughout the writings of Justin Martyr. Indeed, he is conscious that ultimately this may be his own experience. He was right. Yet Justin projected in the second century what would be borne out in the long centuries ahead. Martyrdom has been the ever-present reality for much of the church right up until the present day. During the reign of Emperor Diocletian

(284–305), believers experienced what has been called The Age of the Martyrs. Thousands of Christ's followers died in an empire-wide pogrom that lasted several years.

Throughout the Middle Ages and Reformation period, waves of persecution swept the church. It did not stop there. In Russia (Bolshevik Revolution), China (Boxer Rebellion and Cultural Revolution), Africa, the Sudan, Asia, the Near East, and in dozens of other territories the church has suffered or continues to do so. In the last decade of the twentieth century alone there have been upwards of 150,000 Christians killed globally each year.[8] Such shocking statistics remind believers that Christ promised His church that it, too, would suffer (see Matt. 5:10–13, 39; Luke 6:27–29; John 15:20; Acts 9:5; Gal. 2:20; 1 Pet. 4:13; Rev. 12:11).

As Christians move into the twenty-first century, the reality of global persecution will be an issue with which they will grapple. What is the responsibility of brothers and sisters in Christ to others in the body? What do Scriptures mean that teach about sharing in the sufferings of Christ? What brand of Christianity is demonstrated by apathy and silence, when believers in other countries cry out for tolerance, legal recognition—indeed, life itself? Justin Martyr is perhaps more timely today than ever before for two reasons: He shows the church how to stand to its feet and speak, and he also shows Christians how to die well.

Present-day Martyrs

David Barrett of the World Evangelization Research Center reported, "In one part of the globe, over 10,000 Christians have been killed every year since 1950, due to clashes with anti-Christian mobs, infuriated relatives, state-organized death squads, and so on." The ever-present probability of persecution for many Christians globally demands a response. What will yours be? "Persecuted Christians Today," *Christian History*, vol. 27, p. 36.

CHAPTER 13: CHRISTIANITY AS COMPLETED PHILOSOPHY

In this chapter, Justin spoke of the *logos* a final time, returning to theme of the *logos* who sowed seeds into the thoughts and actions of humankind through the ages. Here Justin called on the philosophers once again to exemplify the picture of God's partial revelation. Each lacks the possession of the full-orbed "hidden understandings and irrefutable knowledge" found in the person of Christ. All of these writers, Justin said, were only able to see realities darkly. Imitation is not the thing itself. Only in Him, who is from the "unbegotten and ineffable God" may philosophy be made complete.

CHAPTERS 14–15: AUTHORIZATION OF WRITINGS

As Justin Martyr closed this volume, he asked the authorities to publish the work, appending what they thought was right, so that people might know what Christians believe. Since all persons judge between good and evil in their own minds, even when they are not in possession of all the facts, Christians are often mislabeled and punished unjustly (ch. 14). If this is going to prevail, asked Justin, why even attempt to have law courts?

Justin's parting shot reminds his readers that these Christian beliefs are more lofty and noble than every human philosophy. They are infinitely better than other poets or historians or playwrights, so there should be no hesitation in making them available. If permission is granted to publish, then these teachings will be broadcast widely that all may read and judge for themselves. He closed with these words, "And from now on we will be silent, having done as much as we could, and having added the prayer that all people everywhere may be counted worthy of the truth. And would that you also, in a manner becoming piety and philosophy, would for your own sakes judge justly" (ch. 15).

"Whatever things were rightly said among all people, are the property of us Christians. For next to God, we worship and love the *logos* who is from the unbegotten and ineffable God, since also He became man for our sakes, that, becoming a partaker of our sufferings, He might also bring us healing. For all the writers were able to see realities darkly through the presence in them of an implanted seed of *logos*. For the seed and imitation of something, imparted according to capacity, is one thing, and another is the thing itself, . . . of which is effected according to the grace coming from Him" (ch. 13).

S̲N̲ COMMENTARY

Closing Argument. In this final passage, Justin closed his plea for a fair hearing, for the debate on Christianity's superiority over paganism, the deficiencies in mythology, the pantheon of deities, and other philosophical systems. He said no more about Christian life and death, of the importance that believers die well. He summed up his arguments with a concise statement of conviction borne of personal experience: Philosophy finds its completion in Christ.

In the final analysis, Justin's concept of *logos*, that unexplainable expression of Almighty God in His Son, the Christ, is the key that unlocks His message. Whether from Platonistic thought, Middle Platonism, Philo, Stoicism, the apostle John, or through the working out of his own theological and philosophical experience, this understanding of Christ as the Eternal Sower of righteousness is perhaps Justin's most lasting contribution to Christian theology. Seldom has one man shaped the history of a people as has this thoughtful teacher.

QUESTIONS TO GUIDE YOUR STUDY

1. What was it about nonbelievers' attitudes toward Christianity that was most difficult for Justin to swallow? Do you have any of these concerns?

2. How did Justin Martyr's experience as a philosopher shape his thinking theologically? Can you pinpoint areas where one informed the other?

3. What is the danger of letting experience dictate/judge theological understanding?

4. Tertullian (c.160–225), African church father, said, "The blood of the martyrs is the seed of the church." What do you think he meant by this statement? Can you see evidence of this truth in the church today?

5. In what ways did Justin Martyr find that philosophy was fully completed in Christ?

DIALOGUE WITH TRYPHO THE JEW

"I am not anxious to exhibit an array of words merely remarkable for its skill; for indeed for this I have not the capacity" (ch. 58).

DATING, AUDIENCE, AND PURPOSE

The dating of *Dialogue with Trypho the Jew* has been the subject of much scholarly debate. The possibilities span two decades of Justin's life, from 142 through 164. All that is certain is that Justin, while living in Ephesus, had a conversation with a Jewish man named Trypho sometime during the Bar Kokhba Wars (132–5?). No one knows exactly when he later recorded it.

He addressed this report of dialogue to his friend, Marcus Pompeius, although he did not include what motivated him to share the results of the conversation. It covers the period of two days, interrupted on the second day when Trypho's friends joined the group. This is evident because Justin repeated himself on the second day in order to include them in the discussion. The break takes place somewhere between chapters 70 and 78.

Bar Kokhba War

A rebellion against Rome (A.D. 132–5) led by Simeo bar Kosevah. His followers called him Bar Kokhba, son of the star. This revolt erupted because the Roman Emperor Hadrian began to build Jerusalem as a pagan city. His plan was to replace the ruins of the Jewish Temple, destroyed in A.D. 70, with one dedicated to Jupiter. The Jews employed guerrilla tactics initially and were able to liberate Jerusalem in A.D. 132. Samaritans and Gentiles joined the Jewish patriots, and the rebellion spread. Hadrian recalled Severus from Britain to restore Roman control. This was accomplished by piecemeal conflict with the insurgents. Bar Kokhba made his last stand in Betar where most of the remaining insurgents died in 135.

This third volume is of a different type altogether from his Apologies. This is the recitation of a second-century interfaith witnessing encounter. It presupposes familiarity, as does all of Justin's works, with classical philosophy. It also relies heavily upon the Old Testament, which Justin holds sacred as the guide for Christian living. For him it is the Word of God, together with the teachings of the apostles, spoken by the Holy Spirit and confirmed by the fulfilled prophecies concerning Christ.

DIALOGUE WITH TRYPHO THE JEW AT A GLANCE

Chapters 1–8	Justin's Personal Testimony
Chapters 9–13	Judaism and Christianity Compared
Chapters 32–129	The Terms *Christ* and *Messiah* Explained
Chapters 130–142	Faithfulness of the Gentiles Upheld

CHAPTERS 1–8: JUSTIN'S PERSONAL TESTIMONY

The opening scene of Justin's *Dialogue* takes place at the Xystus which, Eusebius and Philostratus confide, is the public colonnade in Ephesus where Appolonius normally conducted his disputations. There on the seacoast, as Justin was about to embark on a sea voyage, he met a Jewish man who was immediately attracted by Justin's philosopher's cloak. "Hail, O philosopher!" cried the older fellow, who fell in step with Justin.

They exchanged pleasantries, and Justin discovered that this man is Trypho, a Jew by birth, who escaped the Bar Kokhba War and was spending his days in Greece, primarily Corinth. He also learned of Trypho's sincere, humble search for truth. In fact, Trypho shared that he was taught by Corinthus, the Socratic from Argos, to learn all he could from anyone garbed in a philosopher's robe. Justin took this opportunity to ask why Trypho was searching in philosophy for the truth taught by his own Scriptures? From this point, the conversation was guided by Justin, who shared his testimony first (ch. 1).

These are the source chapters that reveal the most about the private life of Justin Martyr. He recounted the schools of philosophy in which he studied before his conversion. He traced his pilgrimage through Platonism, Stoicism, the Peripatetics, Theoretics, and Pythagoreans (ch. 2). He then shared his conversion experience which took place "in a certain field, not far from the sea." Justin called himself a "philologian," one who either exercises reason or speech and defends philosophy as the path to truth. The old man showed him that philosophy is incomprehensible of complete truth because it is not acquainted fully with God (ch. 3).

Chapters 4 and 5 discuss the soul that can of itself neither see God nor know immortality, both of which find their source in God alone. These sacred things were not known to Plato and other philosophies, the old man explained. The truth was found in the prophets, who both saw and announced the coming Christ (ch. 6–7). In chapter 8, Justin told how the old man left him, never to be seen again. Justin pondered what he had learned. "Straightway a flame was

Formula for a Happy Life

"If, then, you have any concern for yourself, and if you are eagerly looking for salvation, and if you believe in God, you may . . . become acquainted with the Christ of God and, after being initiated, live a happy life" (ch. 8).

kindled in my soul; and a love of the prophets, and of those men who are friends of Christ, possessed me; and whilst revolving his words in my mind, I found this philosophy alone to be safe and profitable. Thus, and for this reason I am a philosopher," he said.

COMMENTARY

Justin's Testimony to Trypho. Dialogue begins with a wonderful picture of lifestyle evangelism. Justin was strolling along a promenade, thinking about his upcoming sea voyage, and was interrupted by questions about truth. Several things come to mind here. First, Justin was quick to recognize the encounter for what it was—an opportunity to share his faith with someone who was open to learning more. Next he took the time to pay attention and to respond. He was a good listener. He did not tell the reader what else he had planned for that day, nor if other appointments were broken, nor even if he missed his ship in the process. What he did reveal, however, was his willingness to hear another's heart longing for God.

Justin also demonstrated the value of a strong personal testimony as a bridge for communicating the gospel message. He told Trypho what his life was like before he was converted, how his conversion took place, and offered the same experience to his new friend. He was vulnerable, eager to share not just the facts but his journey along the way as well. This communicated well; his open frankness touched a responsive chord in Trypho, who felt familiar enough, after interrupting, to stay the afternoon and talk.

Christians today might do well to look carefully at Justin's example here. Many believers chafe at the awkwardness they feel in "going out to witness," as if it must be a dreadful chore. Yet God gives opportunities daily for gentle responses, probing questions, and intriguing answers to all people, fellow Christians and nonbelievers alike. Each encounter with another person holds vast potential for being Christ's "hands, feet, voice, and heart." Like Justin's, a natural, comfortable explanation of one's own experience is often the easiest response to give.

CHAPTERS 9–31: CHRISTIANITY AND JUDAISM COMPARED

At this point in the *Dialogue*, Justin was interrupted in his narrative by Trypho who, with his friends, laugh at Justin's departure from Moses. They think he has transferred his trust from God and placed it in a man of no reputation. Trypho advised Justin to be circumcised, to observe the Sabbath and adhere to the Law. Justin answered this recommendation by offering to prove to Trypho that followers of Christ have not believed groundless stories. The friends responded somewhat rudely to Justin, who suggested that they either listen in silence or leave the discussion. Some of them chose the latter, and the rest of the story took place with Justin, Trypho, and a couple of others sitting down to visit on stone seats in the middle of the colonnade (ch. 9).

In chapter 10, Trypho raised two prongs of a single question: If Christians profess to love and serve God, how can they ignore the given law (Sabbath observances and circumcision) and believe in a human Savior? That Christians live pure and morally upright lives is not the question, he acknowledged. The inconsistency of

Trypho to Justin:

"But it is this that chiefly perplexes us, that you who make a profession of piety, and consider yourselves better than others, do in no respect excel the heathen in your lives; for you do not keep the feasts nor observe the sabbaths, nor practice circumcision, but you put your trust in a mere crucified man, and still, though neglecting God's commandments, hope to obtain good from Him. Have you not read, 'The soul that is not circumcised on the eighth day shall be cut off from his people?' a command which is similarly enjoined as to the stranger, and to him who is bought for money. This covenant you hold in contempt, and yet endeavor to persuade us that you know God, though you perform none of those duties which they who fear Him do" (Trypho, ch. 10).

Justin drew on the Old Testament to support the teaching of a new covenant:

"'The day will come,' says the Lord, 'when I will make a new covenant with the people of Israel and Judah. This covenant will not be like the one I made with their ancestors when I took them by the hand and brought them out of the land of Egypt. They broke that covenant, though I loved them as a husband loves his wife,' says the Lord. 'But this is the new covenant I will make with the people of Israel on that day,' says the Lord. 'I will put my laws in their minds, and I will write them on their hearts. I will be their God, and they will be my people. And they will not need to teach their neighbors, nor will they need to teach their family saying, "You should know the Lord," For everyone, from the least to the greatest, will already know me,' says the Lord. 'And I will forgive their wickedness and will never again remember their sins'" (Jer. 31:31–34, NLT).

belief is what puzzles Trypho. Justin answered, using the Old Testament as his source.

Justin responded to Trypho by saying that there has always been and always will be one God, Creator of the universe. Christians and Jews don't worship two different gods but one and the same God, who delivered Israel from bondage in Egypt. Justin used the language of worship, saying to Trypho that they both adore God.

After acknowledging what they both agree to, Justin pointed out the differences. He said that Christians look to Christ and "a covenant more mighty than all the others" for their hope, while Jews continue to place their hope in the covenant given at Horeb. This law, said Justin, was for Israel only and has now become obsolete. A new covenant and law given in Christ is now valid for all human beings. It is perfect and will last forever.

God does not delight in sacrifices, but has prophesied through Isaiah that sins are forgiven through the blood of Christ (ch. 12–13). Righteousness is not placed in Jewish rites but in the conversion of the heart through Christ alone (ch. 14).

In chapters 15–23, Justin spoke to particular aspects of Jewish worship. Fasting consists in obedience to God; circumcision is a symbol of Israel's hard-heartedness. The Jews caused unrighteousness in other people groups by leading them from the truth, he said. Prescribed meats, the observance of Sabbath, sacrifices and oblations were given to men so they could keep God before their eyes and remain holy unto Him.

Justin then spoke to Christian circumcision, the event in Christ that changes the heart. Jews boast that they are sons of Abraham, said Justin, but base their inheritance on self-justification through works. There is no salvation to the Jews except through Christ.

Trypho asked why Justin quoted freely from the prophetic writings but did not quote the express passages which require Sabbath observance. Justin answered that the Sabbath itself is not as important to God as is an obedient people. For example, were the people who lived before Moses and Abraham, who were not circumcised and who did not observe the Sabbath, commanded to do so by God? "There are so many righteous men who have performed none of these legal ceremonies, and yet are witnessed to by God Himself," he said (ch. 24–29).

Justin went further to claim that the Old Testament is indeed the sacred text of Christians by virtue of the fact that Christians believe them and obey them. Christians possess true righteousness in Christ. Yet if Christ's power be now so great, how much greater will it be at the Second Coming (ch 30–31)! Justin cited passages in Daniel to support this theme of two Advents, the meaning of which he explained in the next section as well.

COMMENTARY

Comparison Between Judaism and Christianity. This lengthy discourse on the differences between two great heritages takes its cue from the question Trypho asked Justin: If Christians profess to love and serve God, how can they ignore the given law (Sabbath observances and circumcision) and believe in a human Savior? This is a valid question. Justin's response comprises not only this section but also the rest of the volume. In part one of his response, however, Justin majored on reinterpreting prophecy and rested his case solely on Scripture. This is to show that the old Law had been replaced with the New Covenant in Christ. His argument began with his claim to believe in the God of Israel. This is a place of common ground for both Justin and Trypho.

Seeking ways to find common ground is always helpful in building bridges with people of other faiths. Justin did this admirably, using his knowledge of their Scripture, which he also claimed as his own, to stand his ground. Even Trypho, who did not agree with Justin's interpretations, could not dispute his scriptural argument, demonstrating that there is no substitute for familiarity with God's Word.

What are some ways we can build bridges with people of other faiths?

CHAPTERS 32–129: TERMS *CHRIST* AND *MESSIAH* EXPLAINED

This is part two of Justin's answer to Trypho's query. Why do Christians worship a human Savior? Justin delighted in the definition of terms this question prescribed. He opened with chapter 32, where he distinguished between the two Advents of Christ. He did this by refiguring the prophet Daniel's number symbols. They point to Jesus Christ, he explained, who is also the fulfillment of Daniel's visions. He suggested that the Old Testament was full of "types" for Christ: Solomon is the Resplendent Reigning Christ; the Psalms figured Him as the Lord of hosts; the fine flour sacrifice represented the Eucharist; and the bells on the priest's robes typified the apostles (ch. 32–42).

In chapter 43, Justin stated categorically that the Law had an end in Christ, who was born of a virgin. He sought to be as persuasive as possible in making his case to Trypho. Justin urged Trypho not to let hardness of heart, fear of the authorities, or false confidence in being a son of Abraham by birth deter him from embracing Christ. Justin followed the Apostle Paul in arguing that those who have the faith of Abraham are Abraham's true heirs (ch. 44–45). In an interesting side note, Justin spoke to Trypho as well as to all Christians in chapters 46–47. His premise was that neither Jews nor Christians who keep the Law contribute to their own righteousness. All true righteousness unto salvation is found in the Son of God.

Here the conversation took a turn when Trypho demanded that Justin prove Christ's divinity: "Resume the discourse where you left off, and bring it to an end. For some of it appears to me to be paradoxical, and wholly incapable of proof" (ch. 48). Beginning with this chapter and continuing through 108, Justin defined the nature of Christ's person, systematically proving His divinity. He addressed His preexistence, Incarnation, death, burial, Resurrection, and Ascension. At the conclusion of this segment, Justin held that belief in Christ is consistent with belief in God alone, thereby proving that Christ and Messiah are one.

Justin began by proving the preexistence of Christ in Old Testament metaphor. Elijah was the precursor of the first coming of Christ; Isaiah predicted John's role as a forerunner of Christ; Jacob predicted two Advents of Christ; Jacob told how Christ would ride on a donkey, and Zechariah confirmed it; Moses predicted the "blood of the grape" and its meaning. Trypho asked to be shown proof without these "types" and metaphors (ch. 49–55).

"All who put their faith in Christ share the same blessing Abraham received because of his faith. But those who depend on the law to make them right with God are under his curse, for the Scriptures say, 'Cursed is everyone who does not observe and obey all these commands that are written in God's Book of the Law.' Consequently, it is clear that no one can ever be right with God by trying to keep the law. For the Scriptures say, 'It is through faith that a righteous person has life.' How different from this way of faith is the way of the law, which says, 'If you wish to find life by obeying the law, you must obey all of its commands.' But Christ has rescued us from the curse pronounced by the law. When he was hung on the cross, he took upon himself the curse for our wrongdoing. For it is written in the Scriptures, 'Cursed is everyone who is hung on a tree'" (Gal. 3: 9–13, NLT).

Justin agreed, answering questions Jews ask of Christ: If He is God, how could He eat? What do Jacob's visions mean? How is Christ distinct from God? What about the figure of Wisdom found in the Old Testament? How can God give glory to another? How can God be born from a virgin? Justin explained all of these puzzles by using the Old Testament. Trypho balked at the onslaught of new information. Justin accused him of bad faith (ch. 56–68).

Justin then changed the subject and told Trypho what he thought about the devil's counterfeit religions found in the myths of Bacchus, Hercules, and Aesculapius. Next he covered Mithraism which, he said, is a perversion of Daniel's and Isaiah's prophecies. Justin then told Trypho how the Jews rejected certain passages of the Septuagint and even removed others from the books of Esdras, Jeremiah, and the Psalms (ch. 69–75).

He returned to the topic of Isaiah's prophecies, centering especially on those dealing with the heavenly things and the millennial reign of Christ. He proved Christ's authority over demons from Psalm 24. Then Justin pointed out figures in the Old Testament that foretell His cross and sending of the Holy Spirit which, he said, Christ "did not receive on account of poverty," or lack of authority in His own right (ch. 76–88).

Trypho had difficulty with the Cross on which Christ suffered and died. It was possible, he said, to believe that Jesus was the Messiah except that the Law cursed anyone who died upon a tree (ch. 89). Justin then cited the places where both the Cross and Christ's death were foretold in Scripture. Both the stretched-out hands of Moses signified it, as did several passages in the Psalms. It is important for the Jews to note that Christ took upon His own body that very curse so that humankind would not have to bear it (ch. 90–100).

Christ is often called "Jacob," "Israel," and "Son of Man." Justin explained how these figured Christ in the Old Testament and how Jonah's story is a type. He told why God permitted His own Son to have experienced human birth and death upon the cross and how the Psalms prophesied the last prayers and Resurrection of Christ (ch. 101–8). He reminded Trypho that the Resurrection did not convert a large number of the Jewish nation but rather caused them to be more strongly opposed to Christ.

This brought Justin to his next point. The conversion of the Gentiles had been prophesied by Micah. A portion of the prophecy had already been fulfilled, and the rest was to take place at the Second Coming of Christ. This truth, Justin said, was proved by the signifying of two goats and other figures in Scripture. The Jews would not accept these, however plainly they might appear. Predictions about Christians abound in Scripture. Justin cited the Malachi prophecies and claimed that Christians are far more religious than Jews. They are the true holy people, called like Abraham and promised to Isaac, Jacob, and Judah (ch. 109–20).

The Jews think that all of these passages refer to strangers or foreigners who live in their midst, said Justin, but this is untrue. Indeed, Christians are the true Israel. Justin spoke of the force the word *Israel* carries and how it fits Christ. Justin was perhaps the first to run down the list of Old Testament authors and their names for Christ, the Word. He explained to Trypho how the Word is not an inanimate power, but is "the

My Name Among the Nations

"'Oh, that one of you would shut the temple doors, so that you would not light useless fires on my altar! I am not pleased with you,' says the Lord Almighty, 'and I will accept no offering from your hands. My name will be great among the nations, from the rising to the setting of the sun. In every place incense and pure offerings will be brought to my name, because my name will be great among the nations'" (Mal. 1:10–11, NIV).

Biblical Knowledge

While reading this section, one begins to realize the shallowness of most Christians' Bible knowledge. Justin's thorough understanding of the Old Testament was astoundingly deep. Perhaps stronger interfaith bridges could be built if Christians better understood their own Scriptures. How believers choose to prioritize their time says what they believe about God. Are the Scriptures truly God's revelation of Himself to humankind? If so, the gauge of one's relationship with God might well be measured by how much time he or she spends alone with Him and with His Word.

person begotten of the Father's substance" (ch. 121–9).

COMMENTARY

Divinity of Christ. The second part of the answer to Trypho's question regarding why Christians worship a human Savior took most of the *Dialogue* to explain. Justin carefully proceeded through the Old Testament, pointing out any prophecy or veiled reference or type or sign or representation of Christ. When he finished, his list was formidable. In the face of such overwhelming evidence, one would expect Trypho to be convinced of Christ's divinity. Justin had forcibly driven home each point. Yet in Justin's mind, the question was not fully answered. Point three was still to come.

CHAPTERS 130–142: FAITHFULNESS OF THE GENTILES UPHELD

The final part of Trypho's question is answered in the closing passages of Justin's *Dialogue*. With chapter 130, he returned to his final argument that the conversion of the Gentiles was foretold. Not just converted, he emphasized to Trypho, but the gospel has flourished greatly among the Gentiles. Justin assured Trypho of God's mercy in Christ, telling him that Christians are praying that Abraham's descendents, according to the flesh, will recognize Jesus for who He is and will respond in faith (ch. 131–3).

The marriages of Jacob tell the story of the Jews and the Gentiles. Children born of Leah, the "weak eyed," are the Jews. Rachel is the mother of the Gentiles. Christ serves both, however, and seeks to recognize children from both marriages with equal dignity. Justin said that in rejecting Christ the Jews have rejected the God who sent Him. By their own choice they have left the Father (ch. 134–6).

Justin maintained that persons who choose wickedness cannot clear themselves by pointing to God's foreknowledge and claiming that they couldn't have chosen otherwise. God has given free wills to men and angels (ch. 137–41).

Trypho and friends rose to leave. He was thoughtful in his response, thanking Justin for such an excellent searching of the Scriptures. He reminded Justin that none of them had been prepared to debate but that they had been pleased with the conversation. If they could do this more often, he said, they might come to a better understanding.

Justin replied that he could do this every day! But since his ship was soon to set sail, he must leave. He encouraged his new friends to "give all diligence" in this struggle for salvation and to give higher honor to Christ than to his present teachers.

His closing word to them was a prayer: "I can wish no better thing for you, sirs, than this, that, recognizing in this way that intelligence is given to every man, you may be of the same opinion as ourselves, and believe that Jesus is the Christ of God" (ch. 142).

 **COMMENTARY**

Faithfulness of the Gentiles. Justin's initial interfaith dialogue turned into a two-day event! Justin's sincerity was evident—his mind sharp and thoughts focused. He claimed not to be well versed at argumentation or polished

What can Justin Martyr teach Christians of this generation about cross-cultural or interfaith witnessing?

speech, yet his passionate plodding over well-traveled ground began to prepare fallow ground for planting. Into the shallow furrows Justin dropped his seeds of truth. He watered it and tended the burgeoning faith that struggled beneath the surface. To his searching gaze no tendrils pushed the sod to find the light.

Yet Justin Martyr, in responding to the opportunity at hand as best he knew how, equipped only with what was in his heart and mind, was faithful with the gospel message. His task was to sow. Knowing that he was not responsible for the harvest, he merely obeyed. In so doing, Justin perhaps demonstrated how his "Sower-*logos*" concept had become reality to him. As a spade in the hand of Christ, he was himself an illuminator of God.

SIGNIFICANCE FOR CHRISTIAN HISTORY

Justin's *First Apology*, *Second Apology*, and *Dialogue with Trypho the Jew*, then, are most significant documents for Christian history. One may conclude this for several reasons. First, they appear within fifty years of the apostolic era, a mere grandfather's span removed from the New Testament period. They comprise, together with a few others, an apologetic link between the era of devotional genre of literature, focused primarily on discipleship and the polemicists' often personal condemnation of both heresies and heretics which follow.

Next, they argue credibly for equal recognition and protection as one among many religious expressions operating in the empire. Readers are able to see firsthand the struggles of the early church to win legal status in that complex cultural milieu of their day. Justin produced clear, cogent arguments for Christianity, based on partial elements of faith that were readily apparent in pagan mythological and philosophical systems. These did not give cause for criminal prosecution for others. How then could Christians be singled out for punishment? These treatises defend the right of Christianity to exist and to be recognized.

Again, Justin's writings demonstrate the superiority of Christianity against contemporary Greek and Roman pantheon and philosophical systems. Using classical philosophical terms, Justin defined Christianity's posture with regard to other beliefs. His primary hook, as he concluded the lengthy comparison and contrast sections, is the righteous living evidenced by Christians. The search for truth, piety, and moral excellence is to be found only in belief in Christ and in obedience to His precepts. For Justin, Christ's sinless life and the moral power of the Christian's witness were both reasonable and self-evident, vaulting the claims of Christianity into prominence.

How would you defend the veracity of the Bible as over against other "sacred writings"?

Another reason that Justin's writings are important is that they are, for the early church, defining documents. They define the theological distinctives which constituted Christianity in the second century. While not supplying the nuances of theological meaning, Justin set forth strong affirmations of the Trinity; God the Father and Unbegotten One; Christ, whom he called the *logos* of God; the person and work of the Holy Spirit, called the prophetic Spirit in Justin's work; the church, and how philosophy relates to Christian expression.

Justin showed how second-century apologists confronted interfaith dialogue. In his *Dialogue with Trypho the Jew*, he displayed a remarkable

What steps do you take in presenting the case of Christian faith?

familiarity with the Old Testament Scriptures and a fine ability to argue from its pages the divinity of Christ. He proved in this manner that Messiah of the Old Testament is none other than Christ, God's Son and *logos*. More than that, Justin revealed his personal testimony, his own journey of faith, and demonstrated how believers can share Christ intelligently with people of other faith traditions.

Justin preserved the earliest full account of a Christian worship service, dating to the mid-second century. He also defined, for both the Roman authorities and for Christians of his day, the manner in which the church conducted its services, how the rites of baptism and Communion were carried out, and the meanings of each ordinance for the believer. This is vitally important, for although addressed to the Roman authorities, his work was perhaps read more thoroughly and often by believers than by pagans.

Thus, Justin provided for the early church an instruction manual, or handbook, of sorts. Writings like these are the only sources of information as to the process by which apostolic Christianity was transformed in doctrine, polity, life, and worship, into the highly sophisticated, powerful, secularized institution of the fourth century.

The above statement takes on new meaning when one realizes that the early church had no known canon of Scripture at the time of Justin's writings. Indeed, the earliest list of New Testament books, accepted about 130, included just the four Gospels and the thirteen Epistles of Paul. Placed on the same footing with the Old Testament listing about 170 to 220, the full sixty-six books were not fully accepted as canonical until almost the year 400. Therefore, Justin's body of work contains critical information as to the early church's usage of the New Testament during the second century. It helps biblical students today understand the process of canonization and how the church viewed matters of doctrine, faith, and practice.

Finally, records such as these challenge Christians today to refuse to be silent. Justin Martyr's work stands throughout the centuries as a clarion call of a single Christian man—student, thinker, teacher, writer, church leader—who found the moment to speak his convictions. This he did, in the face of death.

How can we help ourselves and others be better apologists for Christ?

When the Christian faith is scoffed and degraded; when the divinity of Christ is denied and He is lowered to stand among many gods; when His sacrificial work of redemption is considered merely one of several roads to salvation; when the cross of Christ is either hidden from view or trivialized as an ornament; when humans pass judgment on God, then it is time to stand to defend the claims of Christ.

Justin faced these foes with undaunted courage and died for His Christ in so doing. His stirring testimony of the transforming power of God bears witness that Christianity is indeed the one true faith and philosophy's completion. This, then, is Justin Martyr's legacy to the kingdom and a sterling example of faith giving reasons for its hope.

NOTES

1. Eusebius of Caesarea, *Ecclesiastical History,* 4.11.

2. "The Martyrdom of the Holy Martyrs," *The Writings of Justin Martyr and Athenagoras,* Ante-Nicene Christian Library Series, vol. II, translated by Marcus Dods, George Reith, and B. P. Pratten (Edinburgh: T & T Clark, 1867), 368–8.

3. Leslie William Barnard, *St. Justin Martyr: The First and Second Apologies* in the Ancient Christian Writers Series, The Works of the Fathers in Translation, edited by Walter Burghardt, John Dillon, and Dennis McManus (New York: Paulist Press, 1997), 14.

4. Ibid., 14–16.

5. Taken from footnotes 125–7 from Barnard's Notes to the *First Apology,* 125.

6. See the work of A. Bellinzoni, *The Sayings of Jesus in the Writings of Justin Martyr* (Leiden: E. J. Brill, 1967).

7. The actual number, reported by *World Almanac,* is 1,927,953,000. *World Almanac,* 1997 (Mahwah, New Jersey: Word Almanac Books, 1997), 646.

8. For the latest documentation see the eyewitness accounts of torture and martyrdom in Nina Shea's *The Lions Den* (Nashville: Broadman & Holman, 1997).

SUGGESTED READING

FOR THE LATEST AND MOST HELPFUL TRANSLATION OF JUSTIN MARTYR, SEE:

Burghardt, Walter J., John Dillon, and Dennis McManus, eds. *St. Justin Martyr: The First and Second Apologies* in The Ancient Christian Writers Series, vol. 56. Leslie William Barnard, trans. New York: Paulist Press, 1997. I am indebted to Barnard's excellent critical analysis upon which much of the understanding behind this work rests.

OTHER WRITINGS HELPFUL TO THE STUDY OF JUSTIN MARTYR ABOUND:

Bellinzoni, Arthur J. *The Sayings of Jesus in the Writings of Justin Martyr.* Leiden: E. J. Brill, 1967.

Dods, Marcus, George Reith, and B. P. Pratten, trans. *The Writings of Justin Martyr and Athenagoras.* Edinburg: T & T Clark, 1867.

Roberts, Alexander and James Donaldson, eds. *The Ante-Nicene Fathers: The Writings of the Fathers Down to A.D. 325.* vol. 1. American reprint of the Edinburgh edition. Grand Rapids: Wm. B. Eerdmans Publishing Company, 1953.

FOR PRIMARY SOURCE DOCUMENTATION RELATED TO THE EARLY CHURCH AND CONTEXTUALIZATION OF THIS PERIOD:

Bettenson, Henry. *Documents of the Christian Church.* Second edition. New York: Oxford University Press, 1976.

Kelly, J. N. D. *Early Christian Doctrines.* Fifth edition. New York: Harper and Row, 1978.

Reicke, Bo. *The New Testament Era.* Philadelphia: Fortress Press, 1968.

ADDITIONAL SOURCES:

Cabaniss, Allen. *Pattern in Early Christian Worship*. Macon: Mercer Press, 1989.

Marshall, Paul. *Their Blood Cries Out*. Nashville: Thomas Nelson Press, 1997.

Shea, Nina. *The Lion's Den*. Nashville: Broadman & Holman, 1997.

White, James. *Documents of Christian Worship: Descriptive and Interpretive*. Westminster: John Knox Press, 1992.

Christian History, published by Christianity Today, Inc. Volume 27 deals with persecution in the early church, and volume 37 covers worship during the same period.

图书在版编目（CIP）数据

哪吒传奇.3/ 中国中央电视台编.－北京：人民邮电出版社，2003.6

ISBN 7-115-11424-2

I.哪... II.中... III.动画：连环画－作品－中国－现代 IV. J228.7

中国版本图书馆 CIP 数据核字（2003）第 045306 号

哪吒传奇3

责任编辑：李眉　洪宇　杨晓燕

装帧设计：陈松

北京九金星图形图像技术集团制作

童趣出版有限公司编

人民邮电出版社出版

北京市崇文区夕照寺街 14 号（100061）

北京百花彩印有限公司印制

新华书店总店北京发行所经销

开本：889 × 1194 1/32 印张：3

2003 年 6 月第一版　2003 年 7 月第四次印刷

字数：5 千　印数：100001－120000

ISBN 7-115-11424-2/G・991

定价：9.80 元